Praise for *Fifteen Step*

"Marker expertly explains how the Wall Street inequality machine and our corporate overlords rigged the rules of the economy, distracted the public from the real issues of our time, and fueled the collapse of our middle class. This accessible book helps us reclaim our democracy from its capture and looting by global corporations."

—Chuck Collins
Institute for Policy Studies and author of *99 to 1*

"Marker's brilliant account of how conservatives convinced the American middle class to destroy themselves leads directly to why the Occupy movement had to happen."

—Adam Klugman
Host, *Mad As Hell in America*

"I highly recommend *Fifteen Steps to Corporate Feudalism* for use in the classroom, study groups, and book clubs. The text is well organized and leaves its insights open for political imagination, discussion, and subsequent action."

—Elliot Skinner
Faculty, St. John's College in Santa Fe

"*Fifteen Steps to Corporate Feudalism* accurately traces today's financial meltdown to policies willfully enacted more than a generation ago by the Republican right. The trickle-down theory promised by Reaganomics proved to be a syphoning up, and Fifteen Steps clearly shows that this was always the intention of the perpetrators. A must read for anyone wondering what happened to the American Dream and searching for a guide to restore it."

—Rick Lass
Former secretary, Association of State Green Parties

"When giant corporations are called small businesses, the real small businesses like mine get lost in the rhetoric. This book explains how the right wing has partnered with these giant corporations, causing everyone in local communities to lose ground daily."

—Juan Bernardez
President/Owner, Computer Medics

"Dennis Marker's clear narrative in *Fifteen Steps to Corporate Feudalism* explains how conservatives radically changed the course of American history during the past thirty years. He tells us exactly how they lied to us and got away with it. The country we live in today is their country. Marker asks, at the end of his book, 'What's next?' One step is to read this book and understand the map that got us here; the remaining steps are up to us. The French philosopher Gille Deleuze defines truth as that which opens up the most possibilities. The truths in *Fifteen Steps to Corporate Feudalis* do just that and will keep us moving."

—Linda Hibbs
Cofounder, People for Peace
and member of Occupy Santa Fe

"Dennis Marker does a great job at painting a comprehensive picture of how the financial meltdown was the inevitable result of a carefully planned campaign by the right wing. Easy-to-understand and well organized, *Fifteen Steps to Corporate Feudalism* opens the door to discussion and action."

—Joan Sotkin
Founder, ProsperityPlace.com
and author of *Build Your Money Muscles*

FIFTEEN STEPS
to
CORPORATE FEUDALISM

How the Rich Convinced
America's Middle Class
to Eliminate Themselves

*From Ronald Reagan to
the Tea Party Movement*

DENNIS MARKER

Published by: One Standard Press
PO Box 22690
Santa Fe, NM 87502
www.thefifteensteps.com

Copyeditor: Ellen Kleiner

Book design and production: Janice St. Marie

FIRST EDITION

Printed in the United States of America on recycled paper

Publisher's Cataloging-in-Publication Data
Fifteen steps to corporate feudalism : how the rich convinced America's middle class to eliminate themselves : from Ronald Reagan to the Tea Party Movement / Dennis Marker. -- 1st ed. -- Santa Fe, N.M. : One Standard Press, c2012.

   p. ; cm.

   ISBN: 978-0-9837112-0-9
   Includes bibliographical references.

   1. Middle class--United States--Economic conditions--21st century. 2. Working class--United States--Economic conditions--21st century. 3. Feudalism--United States--History--21st century. 4. Corporate power--United States. 5. Industrial policy--United States--History. 6. Pressure groups--United States. 7. Elite (Social sciences)--United States. 8. Conservatism--United States. 9. United States--Economic policy. 10. United States--Politics and government--2001-2009. I. Title. II. Title: 15 steps to corporate feudalism.

HT690.U5 M37   2012 2012931338
305.5/50973--dc23   1204

1 3 5 7 9 10 8 6 4 2

For my grandmother and soul mate Elvira Edstom Marker,
who taught me to love unconditionally, find joy in all things,
demand justice, believe in myself, follow my dreams,
and ignore those who said I couldn't.

Acknowledgments

I extend special thanks to my wife Diane, for putting up with me all these years. I would also like to thank Meredith Madri, Elliot Skinner, and Linda Hibbs, friends who read the manuscript and encouraged me to take it out of the drawer where it had happily lived, so it could be shared with a broader audience. Finally, I am thankful to Ellen Kleiner and all the others at Blessingway who worked to keep me on task between my trips to Mexico, China, and other ports of call while preparing this book for publication.

Contents

Introduction

For the last three decades, the US middle class has been fighting a losing battle without understanding why. Many Americans have begun working three or more jobs in a desperate attempt to remain financially solvent. But for the majority of Americans the ground is slipping from under their feet. Today, there is little doubt that the US middle class is shrinking. While some claim the US economy remains fundamentally strong and the middle class is doing well, middle-class citizens know they are in trouble. What most do not know, however, is *why* the middle class is disappearing. Many believe it is a combination of bad luck, poor planning, and irresponsible politicians. Why is the US middle class vanishing? Is it simply the by-product of a serious recession? Or is it a result of the reduction of jobs caused by out-of-control government spending, as conservative politicians and Tea Party leaders claim? Could the elimination of the middle class simply be a consequence of an unfortunate miscalculation? The answer to all of these questions is "no." The failure of the US middle class is the direct and intentional outcome of fifteen separate policies first advocated during the Reagan administration and implemented over the next thirty years.

The purpose of this book is to explain how and why the US middle class is being eliminated. It is a guide to understanding the economic collapse of this socioeconomic group, written for the people who are most affected by this change—the US middle class. Let us begin by defining five essential terms that will be used throughout the book.

Feudalism—An economic system in which a nation's people and resources are controlled by a small group of extremely wealthy, powerful individuals, or feudal lords, while the average citizen, or serf, has no recourse to address any wrongdoing or injustice. Historically, feudalism was a system of political organization that flourished from the ninth to the fifteenth century in medieval Europe. Old-style and new-style feudalism work in very similar ways in so far as wealth and resources are controlled by a small group of individuals. The goal of the feudal lords is to continue increasing their wealth and power while sharing as little as possible. In both types of feudalism, the political leaders are beholden to, and therefore controlled by, the feudal lords, and regular citizens are considered to be little more than a natural resource to be exploited at the whim of the feudal lords. Modern-day citizens who are living on a precarious economic edge already share the desperation felt by the earlier serfs, who had no means to escape their impoverished conditions.

Corporate—Anything of, for, or controlled by corporations. In the United States, it is extremely easy and inexpensive to incorporate, resulting in numerous corporations of every imaginable size. In past feudal societies, some people who were not feudal lords owned small amounts of land but had no power, and in today's United States thousands of small corporations have no actual power as well.

Corporate Feudalism—A system in which the owners and directors of a few giant, often multinational corporations exercise the kind of unlimited social, economic, and political power once held by feudal lords. This system diminishes or eliminates the middle class and divides the country into the very wealthy, now known as the 1 percent, and everyone else, the 99 percent.

Middle Class—A socioeconomic group of people occupying a position between the upper class and the lower class, or their standard of living. The United States considers itself a classless society in which everyone between the homeless and the top 1 percent of the wealthiest citizens constitutes the middle class. Within this broad group there are, of course, significant differences between various demographics, such as between the working poor and the top 10 percent. It can be argued that the richest 10 percent are beyond the middle class and the poorest 10 percent are nowhere near it. This broader group does, however, fit comfortably into what the Occupy movement has accurately named "the 99 percent." Despite the differing terminology, one thing is certain: if wealth is allowed to continue being concentrated among increasingly fewer of the richest citizens at the rate it has for the past thirty years, this entire group will be known before long as the *former* middle class.

Conservative—A term referring to individuals who call themselves conservatives, as well as their ideas and policies. While the ideas and policies of many of these self-proclaimed conservatives are, in fact, radical and dangerous rather than conservative, the extreme right-wing in the United States have successfully branded themselves and their policies as "conservative," so this term will be used as currently accepted.

For years now, many Americans have been conned into blaming their own inadequacies for their inability to remain part of the US middle class, a once vibrant socioeconomic group. Today, however, more and more middle-class workers are finally realizing that their economic woes are not their fault. Unfortunately, even as their way of life disappears many other middle-class citizens have been convinced to embrace the very policies that have led directly to the demise of the US middle class over the last thirty years.

These policies were initiated during the Reagan administration. Thirty years ago Ronald Reagan introduced the most radical economic program the United States had ever seen. Then, during successive administrations, conservative Republicans worked tirelessly to get this program passed into law. Finally, during the eight years of George W. Bush's presidency, the program was fully implemented. It involved fifteen steps designed to transform the United States from a regulated middle-class democracy into a corporate feudal republic. Those in power never shared their plan to initiate what can be called Corporate Feudalism with the American public, claiming rather that their agenda would result in great prosperity for the country. However, these fifteen steps did not lead to the prosperity promised. Instead, by the end of George W. Bush's presidency the nation's economy was on life support, and many middle-class individuals who were already falling behind became the newly bankrupt, the permanently unemployed, and the foreclosed upon. While the economic crisis at the end of the Bush presidency resulted in an almost unprecedented change in fortune for the US middle class, it also led directly to some of the largest corporate profits ever recorded and a continuation of tax cuts and other policies designed to benefit people at the very top of the economic ladder.

Not surprisingly, the response of the middle class to this economic turmoil was fear and anger. How this fear and anger were directed was particularly telling. For example, the fear and anger of the failing middle class gave rise to the Tea Party movement. But the policies promoted by the Tea Party movement were nothing more than a rehashing of the same measures that had led to the demise of the middle class in the first place. Such a development was to be expected given the fact that many of the behind-the-scenes funders, creators, and publicists for the Tea Party were the same people who had promoted the fifteen steps leading to Corporate Feudalism for the previous thirty years.

Initially the idea of bankrupting the United States was unthinkable. Now, however, just three short decades later many people believe that is exactly where the United States is headed. This book examines what conservatives claimed would happen when each of the fifteen steps to Corporate Feudalism was implemented. While there is no particular order to the steps that make up the plan for Corporate Feudalism as each step operates independently of the others, they are all necessary for the plan to succeed. We will look at each step separately and review the particular change it proposed. Then we will survey what the conservatives claimed would happen when each step of the plan was implemented. Finally, we will see what actually happened when each change was made and how conservatives subsequently explained the differences between what they said would happen and what really occurred.

At the beginning of our discussion of each of the fifteen steps, readers will be asked to play the game of "what would you do?" The object of this role-playing game is to consider what strategy could best be used to accomplish that particular step in the plan to eliminate the middle class and usher in Corporate Feudalism. Its purpose is to help demonstrate how each step in the plan is perfectly designed to produce the desired outcome.

At the outset, the obvious questions are: What people or organizations were responsible for creating the plan for Corporate Feudalism? How do we know it was a plan at all? The answer to the first question is that the only people who know who created the plan are the creators themselves. It's no secret that the people at the very top level of the world economy have been meeting at different times and places for many years. What they talk about and do is completely secret, however. We can't even find out the identity of many of the people who initially funded the Tea Party, even though it is a public and mainstream movement. As for how we know there was actually a plan for Corporate Feudalism, consider this: If we see a house, a boat, or a car, we may not discern a plan but we know there undoubtedly was one. We can probably visualize a house built without a plan, but it's not a pretty sight. Can we visualize the shift from a middle-class democracy to a corporate feudal republic in the United States without a plan? Is it just a coincidence that at the same time the middle class became unnecessary to the very rich the various policies leading to its elimination were created? Is it possible that the radical economic plan first introduced by Ronald Reagan did the opposite of what it was designed to do but conservatives just kept supporting it anyway? Is it possible that the transfer of wealth from the bottom 99 percent of the population to the top 1 percent in the last thirty years went unnoticed by the people at the top? Certainly anything is possible. But we will see in our discussion of the fifteen steps that each step was a deliberate action with expected outcomes, which had to be hidden from the general public so the middle class would willingly embrace policies calculated to lead to its own demise. When we look at how well all the steps of the plan for Corporate Feudalism fit together to accomplish the goal of eliminating the middle class, it appears more like a finely built castle than the magically unplanned Weasly house of Harry Potter fame.

After thirty years of going largely unnoticed, the rise of Corporate Feudalism in the United States has finally been discovered by a large segment of the American public. It now appears that the Tea Party movement was created and funded by Corporate Feudalists as a pressure release valve designed to focus middle-class anger and frustration away from the true causes of the middle-class demise and any potential solutions not favored by the superrich. In 2010, this misdirected anger and frustration, along with record amounts of corporate cash, were used to elect the most procorporate anti–middle-class House of Representatives in living memory.

In the fall of 2011, the Occupy Wall Street protest placed the focus squarely back on Corporate Feudalists and their political servants. How the Corporate Feudalists and their political hired hands may now try to put this genie back in the bottle and get the middle class to again look elsewhere is unknown. What is known is that before any problem can be solved it must first be understood. If this book helps the middle class understand how and why they find themselves in their current predicament, it will have accomplished its goal.

PART ONE

Some History

CHAPTER 1

Four Charts Every American Should Understand

Middle-class Americans have been intentionally misled and misinformed by politicians and the corporate-owned media for the past thirty years. A visual explanation of what has taken place during this period can be seen in the four charts that follow.

Chart 1 shows that leading up to the present budget crisis Republicans—especially conservatives—have borrowed the most money and created the highest budget deficits. It also demonstrates that the Reagan economic miracle, believed in so

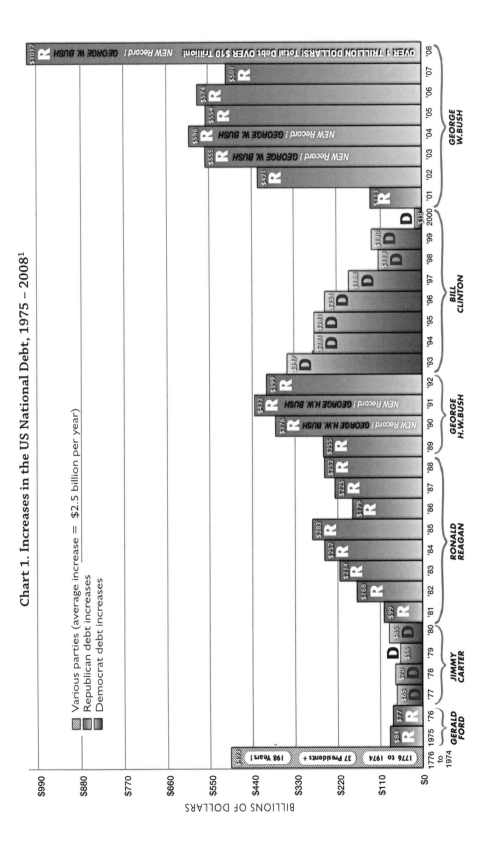

Chart 1. Increases in the US National Debt, 1975 – 2008[1]

Chart 2. The Top 10 Percent Income Share, 1917–2008[2]

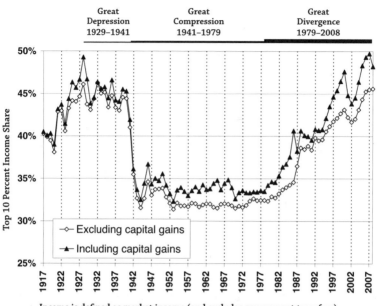

Income is defined as market income (and excludes government transfers).
In 2008, top decile includes all families with an annual income above $109,000.

steadfastly by conservatives and members of the Tea Party movement, was simply a matter of borrowing record amounts of money from future generations to make the economy appear strong.

Chart 2 shows that the income of the top 10 percent of the US population remained relatively constant from the end of the Great Depression until the Reagan Revolution, after which the percent of income controlled by the top 10 percent of the population grew rapidly. The chart dramatically illustrates the saying that the rich get richer while the poor get poorer.

Chart 3 demonstrates that the four hundred richest Americans control as much wealth as the bottom 51 percent of all US households. These four hundred Americans and others in the top 10 percent were the ones who benefited the most when Tea

Party members demanded a continuation of the Bush-era tax cuts for the wealthy.

Chart 3. The Wealth of America's Top 400 Billionaires Compared with That of the Rest of the US (in Billions)[3]

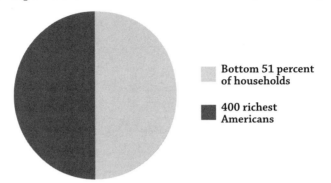

Bottom 51 percent of households

400 richest Americans

Chart 4 illustrates the hourly income of two of the nation's top earners, revealing that for a forty-hour workweek a leading banker is paid $9,000 an hour, while a leading insurance company CEO is paid more than $19,000 an hour. The question we must ask ourselves is whether someone making $19,000 an hour is in need of a massive tax cut during a time of huge national debt, budget cutting, and a generally weak economy.

Chart 4. Breakdown of Hourly Income for a Leading Banker and an Insurance Company CEO in 2008[4]

John Stumpf, Wells Fargo chairman   Ronald Williams, Aetna CEO

Hourly income

Annual income of Wells Fargo chairman—$18 million

Annual income of Aetna CEO—$38.125 million

CHAPTER 2

In the Beginning

A sk yourself this question: If you wanted to destroy the most economically and militarily powerful country the world had ever known, how would you do it? Assuming that you have access to an unlimited amount of money to accomplish your task, there are only two rules you must follow: (1) you cannot attack militarily and (2) you must create your plan focusing on the conditions of thirty years ago when the United States' power and prestige were at their height. However, you do not have to physically destroy the United States; you just have to destroy the middle-class democracy that made the country great.

At this point, you may be asking yourself: Why would anyone want to destroy the United States of thirty years ago?

To answer this question, you have to imagine yourself living and working not only in a different time but under different economic circumstances. Imagine you are positioned at the top of the US economic ladder of thirty years ago. You are incredibly wealthy and powerful. But because of the US middle class and a progressive national tax system, you do not possess the wealth and power you would if you lived in a country without a middle class or progressive taxation. In fact, if you lived in a country with a feudal system you could become a feudal lord with nearly unlimited power and wealth. This might sound pretty good to some people. Fortunately, it is not a temptation most of us have to face. But trying to put ourselves into the minds of the people who made such a choice thirty years ago is helpful for comprehending their motivation. From the outset, it is important to understand that far from being the result of an accident or bad luck the elimination of the US middle class has been part of an extensive and systematic plan by the superrich to remake the United States into a corporate feudal republic. This plan, which has been in effect for more than thirty years, is now beginning to show alarming signs of success.

The proof that the radical change from a middle-class democracy to a corporate feudal republic we are now witnessing is no accident partly resides in the success of the change itself. The only way this change could have occurred so quickly was through the skillful and deliberate implementation of a very specific set of policies. In addition, at each stage of this process results turned out to be the opposite of what conservatives claimed were their goals. With each disastrous result, the conservatives claimed success and continued to support the same policies. For example, when tax cuts for the rich led to ballooning deficits and deteriorating infrastructure, did conservatives call for an end to the tax cuts? No, they called for more. What is interesting is not only that the results of policies were the opposite of those in the stated goals but that each of these policies led the United States in the same direction—away from middle-class democracy and toward a corporate feudal republic. If some of the failed policies promoted by conservatives for the past thirty years had led the nation toward Corporate Feudalism while others had not, it would be fair to give conservatives the benefit of the doubt. But it is impossible to believe that all of the failed policies are the result of an accident when each one of them has led us in exactly the same direction.

Why, one might ask, would a group of wealthy conservatives want to eliminate the middle class and remake the US economy into a corporate feudal republic? To answer this question, we must consider how, over the last thirty years, the redistribution of wealth in the United States from the middle class to the superrich has altered the face of this country. Today, the top four hundred richest people control as much wealth as the bottom 51 percent of the entire US population (see chart 3, p. 6). This is by far the largest disparity in the distribution of wealth of any developed democracy in the world today. With the onset of this change in the fortunes of the richest Americans, have we witnessed any large-scale efforts to correct the imbalance? No. Instead, the newly acquired wealth has led those at the top to hire more lobbyists to create even more laws that favor the rich. This economic imbalance has allowed the wealthiest corporations and individuals to buy elections and politicians, who return the favor with ever more laws benefiting the wealthy at the expense of the middle class.

In short, the more the nation's wealth has been funneled into the hands of the rich, the more it has been used to redistribute wealth to the people at the top. The current economic trajectory of the United States has already severely crippled the members of the middle class and substantially reduced its size so that without immediate modification it will eliminate the US middle class entirely within the next few decades.

Although it may be difficult to believe that a small group of very rich, powerful individuals would have had the foresight to create a plan to make themselves even richer and more powerful at the expense of their country's economic well-being, it shouldn't be. If you are among those who believe we have reached the brink of Corporate Feudalism by accident, consider the odds that the superrich feudal lords-in-waiting could have had such incredible luck to be at the right place at the right time when coincidentally the entire economic system has changed to benefit them at everyone else's expense. How well the steps of this plan, originally put into place during the Reagan administration, have succeeded in accomplishing these ends is persuasive evidence of a conscious effort. Let us now take a look at the plan these very rich and powerful individuals devised and initiated to realize their goal of eliminating the US middle class.

CHAPTER 3

The Plan

Having an idea is great, but an idea alone won't get the job done or guarantee success. Even if the most powerful people in the United States agreed that it was in their best interest to eliminate the middle class and move the country toward Corporate Feudalism, it couldn't just happen without a concrete plan supported by many people. If we examine the substantial strength and wealth of the middle class of thirty years ago, it seems next to impossible to bring the United States to where it is today. But the fact that we can identify fifteen essential steps that worked well together to result in a desired outcome is persuasive evidence of the existence of a well-conceived plan to eliminate the middle class in America, one that was supported by many individuals without their full awareness. While there could have been more than fifteen steps in the plan, if any one of the fifteen steps discussed here had not been implemented, the entire plan would have failed. All fifteen steps were essential, and all worked together.

The Corporate Feudalists designed a plan that would convince the middle class to eliminate itself. The fifteen steps worked in combination to eliminate the political power of the middle class, undermine the traditional role of media, destroy public trust in government, and siphon public money out of government coffers and to the 1 percent. All the while, the Corporate Feudalists were claiming the policies would help the middle class. Each time a law or policy was modified or implemented, the opposite of what was supposed to happen occurred, but these outcomes in no way altered the support the laws or policies received from conservative lawmakers. Instead, their supporters continued to pass laws and implement policies that resulted in the opposite of what the supporters claimed they wanted, and each time one of these laws or policies was passed it moved the nation one step closer to Corporate Feudalism.

Let us consider what would have happened if only some of the steps of the plan had been implemented and only some of the changes had taken place. For example, without a major change in the media that resulted in less accurate or truthful news none of the other changes that led the United States toward Corporate Feudalism likely could have occurred. While prior to the Reagan Revolution, shading the truth might have been tolerated, the media did not tolerate outright lying as happened later. Thirty years ago the major media saw their job as reporting the news. If a politician said A would lead to B, then that is what was reported. If, however, A led to Z instead of B, that would be reported, along with who got it wrong.

More importantly, if a politician was caught telling an outright lie that would also be reported.

Would privatization of government functions have been allowed to continue if the public had found out that it cost millions—or even billions—more taxpayer dollars to turn things over to the private sector? Would deregulation of the banking and mortgage industries have been permitted if the media had informed taxpayers how much they would have had to pay to cover the losses that resulted from fraud and abuse by the private sector? Would our nation have been deceived into entering the second war in Iraq if the media had investigated and reported the dishonest claims of politicians? It is doubtful. The critical change in the way the media reported was essential to success of the plan to implement Corporate Feudalism in the United States.

Let us consider the impact of another step essential to the plan: conning the Evangelical Church. If a conservative Republican propaganda news network had not been established to feed church leaders and members misinformation twenty-four hours a day, church members would have caught on much sooner to what was happening to them and to their families. This, in combination with the elevation of a few multimillion-dollar ministers to conservative political insiders, allowed conservative Republicans to own this group of believers, even as many of the supposedly most righteous conservative politicians and ministers were caught molesting children, picking up men in public restrooms, and stealing from the US taxpayers.

Apart from the existence of a well-conceived, concrete plan, another reason it has been possible to diminish the US middle class is that so many people have taken its existence for granted. The assumption of many was that the US middle class has always been here and always will be. It reminds me of a story my uncle told me about being a young man ordering his first cup of coffee at a diner. After receiving his coffee, my uncle asked how much it cost. The man behind the counter smiled and replied, "Son, coffee costs a dime. It's always been a dime, and it always will be a dime." It's the same with the middle class. Many people believe that it has always been part of the United States and it always will be. Unfortunately, this belief is just as erroneous as the statement about the ten-cent cup of coffee. The middle class was not always here, and there is no guarantee that it will be here in the future.

Anyone who takes the middle class for granted should review the historical facts about the struggle that took place during the transition from agrarian feudalism to middle-class democracy. The inception of an employee-based middle class first occurred as a result of the Industrial Revolution, which began in the latter part of the eighteenth century. Prior to the Industrial Revolution there were people in the middle, including merchants, farmers, and craftspeople working for themselves, who had a status higher than peasant. But for the large majority of people working for someone else some form of economic servitude was the order of the day. During the Industrial Revolution, wealth generated through manufacturing began to replace that generated through land ownership, resulting in a profound shift in economics. At first, the factory owners tried to run their factories in the same way feudal lords ran their lands; namely, the workers were treated like serfs and paid next to nothing for their labors. What changed, however, was the fact that the workers realized the owners needed them. The owners then tried to beat the workers into submission, which led to great labor struggles that lasted many years. In the end, however, a truce was reached—the owners acknowledged that they needed the workers, and the workers acknowledged that they, in turn, needed the owners. Out of this basic agreement, the US middle class was born. Initially it started with establishing fair working conditions and wages, then it soon extended into other areas as well. Union demands increased the power of workers, so, for example, health insurance was provided as an employee benefit. As manufacturing operations increased in complexity, there was a need for more educated workers—administrators, machinists, accountants, and salespeople. As a result, higher levels of public education became essential to the industrialists who were now running the United States. The education caused workers to desire a greater say, not only in their jobs but in their communities and government as well.

This movement organized by educated workers who fought for fair working conditions and wages led to the golden age of the middle class in the United States. No country could compete with the industrial might of the United States during this period. US industrialists were the wealthiest, most powerful people the world had ever known, and the workers shared in their success. Factory workers were able to support their families, educate their children, provide health care for themselves and their families, and even have leisure time to pursue interests other than work. While factory owners were forced to share more of their wealth than they would have liked, they did quite well, as one of the offshoots of a vibrant middle class was the need for more manufactured goods, which, in turn, led to greater profits for manufacturers.

This mutually beneficial relationship between factory owners and workers continued in relative balance and constructive tension for many years. But prior to what was called the "Reagan Revolution" in the 1980s, the world's wealthiest and most powerful individuals realized that the US middle class was no longer required to create vast amounts of wealth. Up until this time, US workers had been needed to make almost all of the products manufactured by US companies for sale in the United States. In addition, thirty years ago US citizens made up much of the market for consumer goods. However, this small group of powerful corporate owners saw that due to just a few changes US workers—the middle class—were no longer necessary. These changes included (1) improvements in international communications; (2) improvements in international transportation; and (3) the introduction of computers and robotic mechanisms. With the advent of these three changes, much of the US workforce was effectively rendered economically unnecessary and politically irrelevant. Unfortunately, what the world's wealthiest and most powerful individuals recognized so long ago has taken the rest of us thirty years to understand.

Let us examine in more detail how these few changes were able to powerfully impact the US middle class. Before these critical changes occurred, the cost of manufacturing goods overseas and shipping them to the United States was prohibitive. Additionally, the communication networks for locations that could provide cheap labor were poor to nonexistent. But in the 1980s this began to shift. International transportation and communication improved to such a degree that it was now possible for goods to be manufactured anywhere in the world and cost effective for them to be shipped to the United States or anywhere else as needed. For goods that remained more cost effective to produce in the United States, computers and machines could handle much of the work, leaving only a few specialized tasks for US workers.

This was all well and good for the leaders of US industry. They could easily imagine the resulting financial rewards of manufacturing their products overseas. There was a big problem, however: US workers would not take kindly to having their jobs eliminated. Changing the country from a fairly well-balanced manufacturing economy to a feudal economy would greatly benefit the few at the top, who would become the new feudal lords, but everyone else would see their lifestyles and dreams for the future severely eroded as they became no more than serfs. Consequently, the question for the Corporate Feudalists was now: How can we eliminate the US middle class without them noticing?

The plan the Corporate Feudalists devised was comprehensive, brilliant, and misleading. In essence, the plan was to get people to believe that black was white and up was down. To succeed at this, they employed the three best motivators known—fear, anger, and greed. Once the Corporate Feudalist plan was developed, what was needed was a world-class salesperson to sell it to the American public. Ronald Reagan was chosen for this position, and he accepted the job. How much Reagan realized about the details of the plan will probably never be known. What Reagan did realize was that many of the radical ideas he introduced as part of the Reagan Revolution produced results that were the opposite of what he claimed. Yet despite this he continued to pitch the Corporate Feudalist policies.

There is no doubt that Ronald Reagan was the perfect pitch man for the job. As an actor, he was accustomed to taking direction and delivering other people's lines. He knew how to project sincerity, anger, sadness, and even surprise on cue. He could, and did, openly lie with the greatest apparent sincerity. He looked and sounded the part of a president. If anyone could convince people that black was white or up was down, it was Ronald Reagan, and that is exactly what he did.

CHAPTER 4

From President Reagan to the Second President Bush

Ronald Reagan's economic policies promoted in the 1980s became known as Reaganomics. Also known as supply-side or trickle-down economics, Reaganomics was like a magic show with Reagan acting the part of the magician. He told us what we were going to see, and then he told us what we were seeing. Just like in a magic show, the impossible appeared to be happening. First, the magician tells us the girl is going to levitate.

Then the magician performs his trick. It sure looks like the girl is levitating, but most people know better and don't really believe in the magic once the show is over.

When Reagan told the American people that he planned to reduce government revenues by cutting taxes for billionaires and millionaires, while at the same time dramatically increasing spending on military hardware and balancing the budget, it sounded like magic. When he told the public his plan was working, many people believed him. Unlike the levitation act, however, after the show ended millions of people kept believing what they had been told. To this day, many otherwise intelligent people believe that Reaganomics actually brought prosperity to the United States, even though it is easy to demonstrate (see chart 1, p. 4) that Reaganomics was a sleight of hand which never paid for itself. Instead, it used massive deficit spending to simulate an economic "miracle."

By the time Reaganomics was implemented, those interested in destroying the middle class had figured out how to let the US government live off the wealth created by previous generations of middle-class Americans, while undermining the middle class itself. Beginning with the Reagan administration, conservatives simply started to rob the US Treasury by increasing debt and deficit spending to pay for their day-to-day operations, maintaining the illusion of prosperity by selling off America's assets and plundering the incredible wealth the United States had accumulated prior to Reagan's election to office. The conservatives even used the perception of wealth to obtain massive loans from foreign countries to further extend the illusion of prosperity while they continued looting the US Treasury and driving the United States ever closer to bankruptcy. It was comparable to someone inheriting a great deal of wealth and squandering it. While the money lasted, everything looked fine. However, as the US middle class started to crumble, people began to look for what was holding up the levitating girl. And by the time anyone started to figure out what had happened, the US Treasury was empty and the US middle class was on life support. By now the manufacturing base necessary to revive the middle class had been dismantled and shipped overseas. All that was left was hope for a miracle called "change."

Since Ronald Reagan was first elected president in 1980, we have had eight years of Reagan, four years of the first President Bush, eight years of Clinton, eight years of the second President Bush, and nearly four years of President Obama. But many of the policies first introduced by Reagan have continued to influence US economic decisions. The radical assumptions Reagan and the conservatives proposed thirty years ago have now been accepted as mainstream by both the media and the public. What is particularly interesting is the fact that during Reagan's tenure many of these ideas were considered so radical as to border on crazy. George H. W. Bush famously called Reagan's economic policies "voodoo economics" before becoming vice president and helping to implement them. What, then, has given these ideas such staying power? It is simply their merit, conservatives claim. Others, however, assert that the successful implementation of the fifteen steps to Corporate Feudalism hid the true costs of these ideas from the American public.

Whatever the reason, since the time of Reaganomics, radical economic ideas—including the deregulation of corporate America, global free trade, and privatization of government services—have been accepted by both major political parties. While Reagan did plenty of damage, including creating the largest national debt in history until George W. Bush took office in 2001, he was able to only partially implement the fifteen steps to Corporate Feudalism because these ideas were viewed negatively during his administration.

From 1988 to 1992, President George H. W. Bush followed in Reagan's footsteps, advancing the fifteen steps as much as possible. However, when the national debt and deficit grew out of hand he raised taxes, forever earning the ire of true-believing conservatives and those interested in eliminating the middle class. When Bill Clinton succeeded Bush in 1993, he continued to support many of the economic policies begun by Reagan and furthered by Bush, to the country's detriment. While Clinton was clearly not a conservative insider, he *was* a conservative Democrat who joined with congressional Republicans to push through the North American Free Trade Agreement (NAFTA). By accepting the global free trade arguments set forth by the Republican conservatives, Clinton put the Democratic seal of approval on one of the most economically destructive parts of the plan for Corporate Feudalism. In addition, Clinton pushed forward the Republican idea of deregulating American business and the banking industry. It was the deregulation of the banking industry that played a major part in creating the subprime mortgage disaster, which led directly to the US housing and economic collapse of 2008.

One of the great successes of the plan for Corporate Feudalism was shifting the current of mainstream political thought far to the right. By filling the government with radical conservative ideologues who refused to compromise, the Reagan administration single-handedly altered the tenor of American political opinion. This shift, in turn, directly influenced how the public perceived Bill Clinton. Prior to the Reagan Revolution's success in changing the US political debate, Clinton would have been considered a conservative Democrat; but by the time he was elected the center had moved so far to the right that he was successfully labeled a liberal, even though he supported large parts of the conservative agenda. This false labeling of Clinton as a liberal afforded cover to the conservatives as they continued to promote the plan for Corporate Feudalism. The resulting narrative that was created emphasized how the untested economic ideas introduced during the Reagan Revolution were supposedly supported not only by conservatives but by "liberals like Clinton" and mainstream Democrats as well.

There is no doubt that the combined presidencies of Ronald Reagan, George H. W. Bush, and Bill Clinton gradually and successfully moved all the elements of the plan for Corporate Feudalism forward. However, to push the plan to the finish line, conservatives needed one more true believer.

George W. Bush fit this bill perfectly. His administration finalized the implementation of all but the bankruptcy step of the fifteen-step plan for Corporate Feudalism, bringing the nation to the brink of bankruptcy during the 2008 financial meltdown. The incremental steps that had been taken prior to George W. Bush's presidency to initiate the plan for Corporate Feudalism were, in effect, given an "adrenaline rush" by his administration. The essence of his presidency was pushing forward the remaining items of the plan for Corporate Feudalism in the name of protecting national security. While many people consider George W. Bush the worst president ever, for the small group of feudal lords-in-waiting Bush was money in the bank—literally and figuratively.

Toward the end of George W. Bush's presidency, however, a problem arose. The conservative agenda created during the Reagan administration had been fulfilled, and the fifteen steps to Corporate Feudalism were nearly complete. The redistribution of wealth from the middle class to the superrich had taken place. Deregulation of the banking sector and real estate markets had all but collapsed the entire US economy and had destroyed much of what was left of middle-class America. At this point, members of the middle class were scared and angry, and where they were about to direct their fear and anger would make a significant difference.

CHAPTER 5

President Obama and the Tea Party Movement

The election of President Barack Obama in 2008 and the ensuing gains for Democrats in Congress could rightly be seen as a major repudiation of conservative governance and the plan for Corporate Feudalism. The 2008 elections were held in the midst of a tumultuous political climate. Leading up to these elections, Republicans had controlled the White House for eight years and, for six of them, both houses of Congress. President George W. Bush had succeeded in remaking the country in the image of Reaganomics and the plan for Corporate Feudalism. Before President George W. Bush left office, the US economy had almost collapsed. This, in turn, led to an international economic disaster that nearly destroyed the worldwide economy—the opposite of what was supposed to happen under Republican rule, as mentioned earlier, and the full implementation of Reaganomics. To prevent a global economic meltdown, President George W. Bush declared that Congress must use taxpayer money to bail out many US and multinational corporations. Fearing a second Great Depression, a majority of Congress acceded to Bush's request.

At this point, the dismal state of the US economy could no longer be hidden from the American public. When Republicans took control of the White House and Congress in 2000, the US budget had a surplus; when they gave up control in 2008, the United States was saddled with both a record budget deficit and a record national debt. In 2000, US job growth was steady; when the Republicans left office in 2008, the nation was facing a greater loss of jobs than at any other time in US history.

These dramatic alterations in the US economy took place in just eight short years. What exactly had changed during that time? For one thing, the Republicans had pushed through massive tax cuts that benefited the wealthiest Americans. In addition, while they were in control of the White House and Congress, Bush and the Republicans had started two wars that exponentially increased the national deficit. The Bush administration intentionally hid the actual cost of these wars from the American public by keeping their cost off the budget, enabling the administration to make the budget deficit seem much smaller than it actually was.

Another factor leading up to the financial crisis of 2008 was the continued deregulation of banks and insurance companies initiated during the Clinton administration. This deregulation, combined with a conscious effort not to enforce existing regulations, allowed large multinational corporations to do just about anything they wanted to increase their profits.

Enter the Obama administration and the attendant launch of the Tea Party movement. The primary objective of the Tea Party leadership, funders, and Fox News publicists was to convince a fearful, angry middle class that Obama and big-spending Democrats had caused the economic collapse of 2008. The Tea Party blamed Obama and the Democrats for the record deficits and national debt created during the administration of George W. Bush, which included six years of a Republican-ruled Congress. Using massive—but unknown and untraceable—amounts of corporate money, the Tea Party movement successfully convinced large numbers of angry, frightened middle-class Americans to think they were voting for fiscal discipline by returning the Republicans to power in 2010. When the Tea Party onion is peeled back, however, it is not surprising to see that much of the seed money that set the Tea Party in motion came from some of the richest corporate billionaires in the world. In addition, behind-the-scenes leaders of the Tea Party movement included some of the best-connected conservative politicians and corporate lobbyists. Most importantly, however, there could have been no national Tea Party movement without the 24/7 organization and free publicity provided by the propaganda wing of the Corporate Feudalists known as the Fox News Network.

Ultimately the only reason the Tea Party movement came into being was in response to the successful implementation of the fifteen steps to Corporate Feudalism by George W. Bush's administration. Without this success and the resulting change in fortunes of the US middle class, there would have been no need to direct the pent-up middle-class rage away from the Corporate Feudalists, and the Tea Party movement would never have been born.

In the fall of 2011, a radical change took place in how middle-class citizens perceived themselves and their plight. After thirty years of watching their political and economic status decline, they began to say enough is enough and protest the disparity of wealth among parts of the American population. It started with a small number of people deciding to occupy Wall Street, the symbol of American corporate wealth and scene of the greatest unprosecuted crime against the middle class in US history. Within a few short weeks, the Occupy movement had become a nationwide phenomenon. Unlike the Tea Party movement, which was secretly funded by corporate giants and lobbyists like the Koch Brothers and Dick Army, the Occupy movement was a grassroots leaderless expression of the people, by the people, and for the people.

While the Tea Party movement was given unprecedented news coverage on the Fox News Network before it existed, the Occupy movement at first received little news coverage. As it grew in size and sprang up in more locations, much of the corporate media began to scorn and ridicule the movement, calling its participants leaderless, directionless, communist, socialist, dirty, lazy, and hippies. However, the Occupy movement was in no way deterred by this negative portrayal, aware that it reflected the circumstances of America's middle class.

Before the Occupy movement began, almost all the anger of the middle class had been directed away from the Corporate Feudalists and their political supporters due to clever marketing and well-funded public relations campaigns. There had been little publicized resistance to the move from middle-class democracy to a corporate feudal republic. Wisconsin Governor Scott Walker almost single-handedly created a movement against his state's anti-union procorporate activities, mobilizing people throughout the United States. But nationally, Republicans had managed to control the debate while demanding cuts for all programs that helped the middle class and stridently insisting that tax increases for millionaires and billionaires were "off the table." As a result of these successful efforts by Republicans, there was very little talk about how middle-class wealth had been systematically transferred to the top 1 percent of America's households and even less about what had happened to America's middle class.

With the advent of the Occupy movement, the discussion changed radically. Thirty years of conservative insistence that "we are all in this together" was washed away with the simple decree "we are the 99 percent." Almost instantly, the members of the US middle class were exposed to the reality that they had been losing ground to the top 1 percent—not because of anything they had done but because the deck had been stacked against them by unfair laws and policies written for the rich by the rich and passed by politicians bought and paid for by the economic giants of America.

How the Corporate Feudalists will attempt to stop this movement is unknown. They tried ignoring it, which didn't work. They tried ridiculing it, which likewise failed. Arrests and excessive police force were used, also to no avail. But the Corporate Feudalists did not achieve their prestige by playing nice or being fair, so they will no doubt introduce new schemes to destroy this movement before it endangers their privileged status.

Now that large numbers of middle-class citizens are being exposed to the reality of America's struggling 99 percent, it's time to examine how the middle class was brought to this desperate situation. One thing is certain: to fix the problem, we first have to understand how we got here.

PART TWO

The Fifteen Steps

CHAPTER 6

Step One: Controlling the Media

Since controlling the media had a great impact on many of the other steps to Corporate Feudalism, this is where we will begin our investigation.

First, you will be asked to consider what you would do to accomplish this step—a question that will be posed for each of the fifteen steps. To answer, you will need to adopt a mindset of thirty years ago, when the middle class was at its peak, the economy was strong, and citizens of the United States were full of optimism. Remember, you will have unlimited financial resources at your disposal to help you accomplish these steps. In each case, see if your plan is as effective as the one the Corporate Feudalists implemented.

Regarding step one, what you would do? Your goal is to figure out how to gain control of the media without anyone noticing. If you want to control a country without resorting to military force, you *need* to control its media. Dictatorships understand this concept and consequently exercise complete control over their media sources, assuming the ownership and operations of all television and radio stations, and newspapers. Anyone caught publishing unofficial media reports is jailed or otherwise punished for going against the official government line.

While this kind of absolute media control may work for dictatorships, the United States of thirty years ago was not a dictatorship. Therefore, how does a small group of people with unlimited financial resources take control of a supposedly free media? This was the question conservatives faced thirty years ago. Their answer, like everything else in their plan, was brilliant: once Ronald Reagan was elected, the conservatives used his popularity to begin destroying the free media in the United States. Gradually, without anyone noticing, the Reagan administration completely changed the laws and regulations guiding media coverage in the United States and altered the public's view of the media.

Reagan looked good, and he knew how to use the media to his advantage. Nevertheless, his staff and operatives began putting new and far more restrictive rules into place regarding his media appearances and those of his administration. Media access to Reagan and his administration was, up to that time, the most tightly controlled in US history. Only people providing positive coverage were given the exclusives that had previously been granted to all the major news outlets on a somewhat equal basis.

More importantly for purposes of controlling the media, a separate office was created to monitor all news and information concerning the administration and its interests—the Office of Public Diplomacy, or OPD, headed by conservative ideologue Otto Reich. The primary purpose of this office was to monitor news reports and follow up with the media if reports were not to the administration's liking, to ensure that the Reagan administration was receiving positive coverage. For example, if a particular reporter stated something unfavorable about the administration, the reporter would first receive a phone call from the OPD. If the phone call proved insufficient to pressure the reporter to cease the unfavorable coverage, it would be followed by a visit from an OPD official. The pimary enforcement method used by the OPD to make sure a reporter got back on track was the threat of being left out of the loop, which meant that a reporter would lose any chance of exclusives or private briefings. In addition, the reporter would not get called on at press conferences and other staged media events. In a very short time, these two tactics alone would lead to a downgrading of the reporter's value within the news organization.

Imagine that you are a reporter specializing in national politics and White House coverage for *Newsweek* magazine and your primary competition is *Time* magazine. If the Reagan administration decided to punish you, they might reward the reporter from *Time* with an invitation to a private briefing that you don't receive. Consequently the reporter from *Time* gets a good story that you miss. At press briefings, the *Time* reporter is called on, but you are ignored. Soon your editor notices that your competitor at *Time* magazine is acquiring much better information than you and has better access to news sources.

At some point, your editor may decide to make a staff change, as the magazine cannot afford to be outdone by its rival in something as essential as this area of coverage. Aware of such a possibility, you could either start providing positive coverage of the administration or accept that you might be transferred to a place where you can get the job done—Central Africa, perhaps.

Further, the OPD did not limit its calls and visits to reporters. If a reporter remained unresponsive, editors and producers received calls and visits, as well as publishers, owners, and anyone else who exerted influence over the reporter in question. In one case I was told of personally, top executives at National Public Radio (NPR) received a visit from Otto Reich because a particularly damaging report had been aired about a massacre that had taken place in a rural village in El Salvador. When the meeting between Reich and NPR had been arranged, the assumption of NPR officials was that Reich had information placing the accuracy of the story in question. However, what officials discovered was quite different. Reich had no information that challenged the accuracy of the story, nor did he pretend to. Instead, he simply claimed that the story had harmed US national security. Reich also let it be known that if this kind of anti-administration reporting continued, the Reagan administration would be forced to consider eliminating government funding for NPR. This was the ultimate threat. While NPR executives would not admit that the Otto Reich visit actually changed their reporting on El Salvador, they did admit that the visit was chilling, and subsequently there were no more NPR stories graphically reporting Salvadoran government massacres, although the massacres continued.

Another tactic the Reaganites used to control the media was to openly attack them for their supposedly liberal bias. This resulted in several positive outcomes for the conservatives.

First, it deflected attention from the policies covered by the media. Second, it forced the media to be more "balanced" in their reporting. In the end, forcing the media to be "balanced" proved to be one of the greatest methods of controlling the media in the United States and completely altered the standards for national reporting. Prior to the balance standard, the truth standard had been used; namely, a reporter's job was to uncover the truth and report it. After the balance standard was adopted, a reporter only had to find two sides of a story.

Let's look at an example of "balanced" reporting. If a reporter was focusing on a story about whether a husband had beaten a wife, in keeping with the truth standard the reporter's job would be to find out if his wife had actually been beaten and to report whether or not the charge was true. However, using the balance standard the reporter only had to report the charge and the denial if there was one. While the balance standard was in some respects much easier for a reporter, it was also much less helpful to the public. Now a person could watch the news or read a newspaper and have no idea what actually happened. They would simply learn of a charge and a countercharge.

Once the balance standard took hold, the media were controlled by whoever had the best media operation. Because the conservatives understood what was being done to change the media, they were prepared with exactly the type of media operation needed to implement this new standard. For purposes of "balanced" reporting, all that was needed was amplification and repetition. And the Reagan White House easily provided the amplification and the repetition.

To better understand how this works, consider that everything a president says is news whether or not it is true. As long as you know the media are not going to report that you are openly lying, you are free to say whatever you want. You can take any issue and state what you claim to be the facts. A reporter who has time to call someone with a different perspective may report both sides. Then the next day the president or someone else in the administration can repeat their version, or several people in the administration can make the same claim at once. A reporter who has time to obtain a balancing quote from someone else may make the effort to do so, or may not; after all, the reporter related a different perspective yesterday. This sequence of events can happen over and over again until a president's version of events is believed as fact, whether or not it is true. Alternatively, if the reporter continues to find opposing quotes, the reporter or a superior may receive a dreaded call from the OPD. Either way, the president is able to control the facts simply by insisting that his version of events is true. The reporter does not dare to call him a liar. The consequences are too great.

Thirty years ago the Democrats were unwilling to call the president a liar even when they knew he was lying. This was partly because blatant lying to the media was a new concept. Democrats might have simply concluded that if President Reagan was so insistent and the media kept reporting his version of the story as true maybe there was some truth to it.

There was yet another reason why the Democrats refused to call Reagan a liar and the conservatives were able to take full advantage of it during the Reagan administration. Prior to the plan for Corporate Feudalism, both the Democrat and Republican parties had maintained a civility that prevented them from calling each other names, especially liars. However, because the Republicans were writing new rules with regard to the media and reporting, and the Democrats didn't know what the new rules were, the Republicans had free reign to manipulate the truth, which they did again and again.

Another successful tactic used to control the media in the United States was deregulation. Prior to the Reagan Revolution, there were firm guidelines restricting the number and types of media a single entity could own. The conservative strategy was to eliminate these regulations and place the majority of all US media in a very small number of extremely wealthy hands to effectively eliminate competition and make certain the same story was told by every media outlet. Deregulation made it possible for conservatives to control a handful of large media corporations, which was much easier than trying to control many hundreds of independent media outlets and owners.

The final stroke of genius leading to control of the US media involved eliminating the Fairness Doctrine. Introduced in 1949, the Fairness Doctrine prevented any media source from using the publicly owned airwaves as a propaganda tool for a particular side or issue. Where there were differences of opinion and no clear provable facts on one side or the other, the Fairness Doctrine required that both sides of an argument be presented.

With the Fairness Doctrine in place, it was impossible for a one-sided propaganda machine like the Fox News Network to exist. Once the Reagan administration removed the Fairness Doctrine in 1987, however, any group or individual with enough money could buy the public airwaves and report any-thing they wanted. If they wanted to tell only one side of a story or openly lie, they could, since it was no longer necessary for opposing views to be given equal or, for that matter, any air-time. For the first time in US history, it was possible to openly propagandize using the public airwaves. All that was required was an incredible amount of money to buy and operate media outlets. The combination of OPD pressure used to get favor-able coverage, introduction of "balanced" reporting, media deregulation, and end of the Fairness Doctrine completely gutted what had previously been one of the world's most vital media operations.

In addition to gaining unprecedented control of the media through these tactics, conservatives began a systematic campaign to destroy the public's faith in the media. This was done by continually attacking the media as liberal, biased, dishonest, lazy, and anything else that would drive a wedge between the media and the American public. The goal of this part of the conservatives' strategy was to minimize or eliminate the impact of any news coverage deemed inconsistent with the goals of Corporate Feudalism. Any time a news story that contained facts contrary to the conservative line was printed or aired, it was attacked and dismissed as "liberal bias," even if the story was 100 percent accurate.

Once conservatives managed to convince the public that real news could not be believed, there would be no way for the general public to discern what was actually happening in either the country or the world. If the truth were called a lie and the people reporting the truth were attacked as liars and dupes, there would be no way for voters to make informed decisions. And if voters are unable to make informed decisions based on actual facts, the entire democratic system fails since one of the fundamental principles of democracy is that people have a choice based on facts, and that an independent media provides those facts. This would prove the point that Thomas Jefferson made when he said, in many different ways, that there could be no democracy without an accurately informed public. If a politician claims to be working for a particular issue and then actually works against it, the news media can expose the disparity; but if people are taught to distrust the news media, then the politician can more easily convince the public that the report is not true, even when the media are doing their job.

Thirty years of systematic attacks on the media have resulted in making the public wary of what they read or hear on the news. This general distrust of the media has allowed conservatives to convince many voters to support policies that are the opposite of what voters think they are supporting, including the policies promoting Corporate Feudalism. In addition, the creation of full-time conservative propaganda machines like the Fox News Network and conservative talk radio have played a dramatic role in moving the United States toward Corporate Feudalism.

Did you come up with a better way to gain political control of the mainstream media than the one the Corporate Feudalists used? Or do you believe the plan they used was the most effective one available?

CHAPTER 7

Step Two: Rush Limbaugh and "Foxaganda"

What would you do? Your goal for this step is to develop a media empire poised to convince millions of people that what you say is true, even when it can be proven false—to create an alternative reality that will convince people that up is down and black is white. Remember, according to the rules of our game you have access to unlimited financial resources.

While acquiring control of the mainstream media was essential to the Corporate Feudalists, persuading people to distrust the mainstream media and then establishing a media empire with the power to create an alternative reality in the American public's mind was even more important. This propaganda operation had to be extremely effective and available twenty-four hours a day, so that people could always tune in, regardless of their schedule, and never need to look elsewhere for their news. These days it is hard to remember a time when conservatives were not in control of their own media empire. Thirty years ago, however, there was no right-wing television network or nationally syndicated hate radio. So what the Corporate Feudalists did was create their own separate—but very unequal—media empires. The scope of what they managed to accomplish through these media empires is nothing short of breathtaking. They did, of course, have several advantages. For one thing, the Corporate Feudalists were protected by one of the nation's favorite inventions—the myth of the American free press. While the United States does have a free press, it belongs to the highest bidder. News that favorably impacts the corporations owning America's free press and airwaves is always given a more sympathetic hearing than news that opposes these interests.

Another advantage was that in the United States money is connected to credibility, and thus if a new media empire is created that appears to be flush with cash, it is assumed to be credible. This credibility based on money allowed the Corporate Feudalists' propaganda machine not only to come into play but to operate largely undetected for nearly thirty years.

Perhaps the most significant reason the Corporate Feudalists were able to get away with creating their own propaganda empire in the midst of the real media was that it had never before been done. Prior to the Reagan Revolution, no private interest group had ever established a propaganda machine with resources that matched those of the real news outlets. So no one expected it.

The formation of the Corporate Feudalists' propaganda empire started with Rush Limbaugh, the undisputed king of American talk radio. The format of *The Rush Limbaugh Show* reflected nothing less than the new conservative agenda—or, more specifically, the plan for the shift to Corporate Feudalism. Limbaugh was outrageous, bombastic, confident, definite, and extremely entertaining. But his most significant characteristic in terms of Corporate Feudalism was a complete disregard for the truth. Whether or not he started out working for them directly, his agenda was the same as the Corporate Feudalists', and he promoted their views relentlessly. Limbaugh's agenda never wavered, nor was it influenced by something as dull and unentertaining as the truth.

Starting at the time of the Reagan administration, Limbaugh and the conservative movement realized that they were not confined by reality, and Limbaugh knew that his listeners would believe him no matter what he said, as long as he remained consistent and spoke powerfully and authoritatively. Limbaugh could sell anything, and people who provided facts that countered his claims were simply dismissed. His listeners' loyalty stemmed, in part, from the fact that he had an answer for everything. He never entertained doubts or explored gray areas. For many people, the temptation of easy answers was compelling. Here was a person who could tell the US middle class exactly what was happening and why. Committed listeners felt like insiders. When caught in an outright lie, Limbaugh just kept repeating the lie, and his listeners believed him. Then comedian and now senator Al Franken wrote an entire book dedicated to Limbaugh's lies, and during a special segment of his radio show examined specific lies Limbaugh had told the day before. But ultimately Limbaugh owned his audience, and no amount of fact-checking could sway his loyal followers.

In Limbaugh's world, all the pieces fit together like a house of cards. You had to believe that the global free market would regulate itself. You had to believe that cutting taxes for American's wealthiest citizens would somehow benefit the middle class. You had to believe that allowing companies to ship American jobs overseas while sending products back to US consumers duty-free made sense. If you questioned any of this, the entire theory would fall apart. But for his committed believers it was persuasive and the house of cards stood.

The first nationwide propagandist with a daily radio program the country had ever heard, Limbaugh has probably done more to convince people to eliminate the US middle class than any other individual. He accomplished this by supporting policies that benefited the wealthiest Americans at the expense of the middle class, while convincing his listeners that the policies and people attempting to help the middle class were its enemies. Perhaps because he was the first such national propagandist, intelligent people tended not to notice his impact, even though many of his statements were provably false. The assumption was that although his listeners were entertained, they were not influenced by him. But by the time those who underestimated his influence realized the depth of his impact, it was too late.

However unwittingly, Limbaugh's network of loyal listeners swelled the base of people committed to the plan for Corporate Feudalism. The real coup, however, was the Fox News Network, or "Foxaganda,"* which turned out to be even

---

*Throughout the remainder of this book, the Fox News Network is referred to as "Foxaganda" because otherwise the use of its self-given name may give the impression that its programming is "news," which it is not. The Fox News Network does not report real news but rather broadcasts conservative propaganda.

more influential than Limbaugh. While the Limbaugh faithful believed him in the face of evidence to the contrary, he made factual errors too often and was too obnoxiously abrasive to be accepted by a more mainstream audience. In addition, Limbaugh was only a one-man propaganda operation. He could teach his listeners how to interpret other news and tell them what to believe, but he could not be all the news all the time. Even his most ardent followers needed to obtain more detailed news from other sources. The Foxaganda Network was created to fill this vacuum.

When Foxaganda was established by billionaire conservative Rupert Murdoch and Republican political strategist Roger Ailes, many people noticed it had a distinctly conservative bent, but they assumed it was still real news. The best lies always have some relationship to the truth, and Foxaganda used this fact to its advantage, delicately walking the fine line between truth and falsehood. Actually, Foxaganda had a far more complex agenda than simply reporting the news. It created news regarding issues involving the conservative or Corporate Feudalist agenda, using the same playbook as Rush Limbaugh.

While the mainstream news media was sometimes right and sometimes wrong, its political slant varied. At times the reporting would favor the liberals; the next day it would support the conservatives. At times an interpretation came from what made sense to a reporter, and often it was based on a relationship with someone. Although the Reagan administration had proved it was possible to influence or even intimidate the mainstream news outlets, for all their faults they still reported the real news. However, from day one Foxaganda was a very different animal. It had a specific agenda and coordinated directly with media people from the conservative movement, including those holding political office. Its agenda was to claim fairness and accuracy while serving as the propaganda arm of the conservative wing of the Republican Party and the voice of the Corporate Feudalists. Twenty-four hours a day, Foxaganda consistently presented the conservative agenda as fact, claiming it was simply countering a liberal bias from the other networks. In truth, this liberal bias did not exist. What did exist was a procorporate, probusiness bias, the one thing shared by both the real media and Foxaganda.

The result of the ideological conflict between Foxaganda and the real news was somewhat predictable. The conservatives had a well-financed, twenty-four-hour-a-day network committed to selling their agenda as news. The moderates and liberals, on the other hand, had to try to get their views covered on the real news, which sometimes agreed with them and sometimes agreed with the conservatives. It was not a fair fight.

With the creation of Foxaganda, the Corporate Feudalists had exactly what they needed—a presumed news source that operated twenty-four hours a day. If they could convince people to watch Foxaganda exclusively, they could easily build the base they needed to destroy the middle class. And that is what they did. As a result, Foxaganda became the greatest organizing tool for conservative causes the United States had ever seen. Political arguments that ultimately led to the decline of the middle class were presented as fact, and Foxaganda became the most powerful and influential mouthpiece for Corporate Feudalism. Every day, viewers heard about the wonders of such aspects of the conservative agenda as deregulation and unrestricted global free trade. Viewers were being taught how and what to think, while they assumed they were watching real news.

Although at the time it was easy to miss what the Corporate Feudalists were doing with Foxaganda, today it is clear, and the success of the Foxaganda propaganda operation cannot be overstated. The number of middle-class people committed to policies that could lead to the elimination of the middle class and the return to feudalism has grown substantially. The 27 percent or so who clung to supporting the Bush administration until the bitter end were probably exclusive Foxaganda watchers, as are the people who still believe Saddam Hussein had something to do with 9/11 or that Al Qaeda was operating inside Iraq before the Bush invasion.

The most damning proof of Foxaganda's corrosive impact on the US middle class came in several studies, including a 2010 University of Maryland investigation that found Fox News viewers are much more likely than others to believe false information about American politics and an even more damaging 2011 Fairleigh Dickenson University study that found Fox News viewers to be less informed than people who watch no news at all. In fact, Foxaganda's greatest success may be its creation and sale of an often completely false package of information. Like the missing weapons of mass destruction used to justify the unnecessary war with Iraq, Foxaganda's "facts" are found exclusively at the Fox News studio and nowhere else in the world.

Yet another huge impact of Foxaganda is how it has influenced the real news media. Because Foxaganda's credibility was built upon its wealth, other networks have been influenced by what Foxaganda reported. The most important influence came about when Foxaganda called the Florida presidential election for Bush in 2000. Other networks had begun calling Florida for Gore based on the exit polls—polls which, until that election, had always been considered reliable. But then Foxaganda called Florida for Bush, and Foxaganda was definite in its call.

What did Foxaganda know? There are two possibilities. One possibility is that Foxaganda knew nothing when it called the election for Bush on that famous election eve. The second possibility is that it had advance knowledge of the number of legitimate votes for Gore that were being thrown out, or of the more than fifty-five thousand legitimately registered Democratic voters who had been illegally "purged" from the voter rolls before the election. In either case, it can be demonstrated that if Foxaganda had not called Florida for Bush, Gore would have been elected president. It was the initial Foxaganda report on election night that threw the entire election into chaos—a significant impact, especially considering that George W. Bush ended up overseeing the greatest rise in the US deficit and the greatest transfer of wealth from the middle class to the superrich.

Profoundly influenced by the Foxaganda network, the 2000 presidential election was an essential part of the plan for Corporate Feudalism. While Ronald Reagan introduced all of the elements of the plan, and both President George H. W. Bush and President Bill Clinton were able to slowly move the agenda along, the election of George W. Bush led to the wholesale implementation of the plan. This, in turn, resulted in the near bankrupting of the United States and rapid move toward the elimination of the US middle class.

While it is true that all fifteen steps were necessary to bring about Corporate Feudalism and the elimination of the US middle class, it is also fair to say that the creation of the propaganda network started by Rush Limbaugh and carried out by Foxaganda was the glue that held the entire operation together. Day in and day out, Limbaugh and Foxaganda presented an alternative reality for the American public, providing cover each time the opposite of what conservatives promised came true. This propaganda network convinced honest people that the obvious personal immorality of so many conservative political and religious leaders was nothing compared to the supposed evil of the godless liberals.

Even after the US economic order has nearly collapsed, due in large part to the plan for Corporate Feudalism, Foxaganda and Limbaugh still work every day to convince their committed audiences that the nation's economic woes and the demise of the middle class are really the liberals' fault. Unfortunately, the other news networks continue to include Foxaganda's conservative analysis—however discredited—so as not to seem biased themselves.

Did you think of a better way to convince middle-class people to support policies that transferred their wealth directly to the top 1 percent than creating your own twenty-four–hour propaganda network? Or did you conclude that the plan used by the Corporate Feudalists was the best one available?

CHAPTER 8

Step Three: Destroying the Unions

What would you do? Your goal for this step is to convince the middle class that unions are their enemy. You may use the unlimited financial resources you have, but remember that unions can be influential if they have an equal say, so part of your job is to make sure they do not have a voice.

Prior to the formation of the unions there was no employee-based middle class, and there will be none once the unions are gone. Try to find a country anywhere that has a vibrant middle class without labor unions. There is none. It is not likely that this is just a coincidence.

To demonstrate the significance of the unions, let us take a brief look at US history. When wealth started to be created from industrial enterprises rather than land-based ones, people with landholdings began establishing factories. Because these landowners controlled the majority of the nation's wealth at the time, as factory owners they attempted to maintain the same type of wage structure previously used for their land-based enterprises—paying as little as they could get away with, even hiring children when possible.

When workers first began to organize in an attempt to secure fair wages and safe working conditions, they were treated harshly by factory owners. Then, as now, those at the top had a controlling interest in the politicians who ran the government, so the power of government was used to disrupt workers' attempts to organize. After inflicting tremendous hardships on the workers to suppress their efforts to organize, it was determined by those in power that fighting these work-ers was a losing battle. So workers were allowed to unionize, and it was unions that fought for the rights the middle class now take for granted—from child labor laws to the forty-hour workweek, health care, and public education.

From the time unions were established until the beginning of the Reagan Revolution, the goal of middle-class workers everywhere was to attain the type of wages and benefits received by union workers. The success of the unions con-vinced many employers to offer nonunion workers the same type of wages and benefits provided to union workers.

Now, if your goal was to eliminate the middle class you would have to get rid of—or at least significantly weaken—the unions. Not surprisingly, that was one of the main goals of the Reagan Revolution, and it continues to be one of the goals of the Republican Party and the Corporate Feudalists. The strategy used to weaken and destroy the unions was the same one implemented for other parts of the plan for Corporate Feudalism: a combination of distorted information and outright lies. The Corporate Feudalists carefully employed the language of the middle class to promote their arguments and to teach middle-class workers to despise the unions. This campaign was publicized and treated as fact by the national news media, which, while being sometimes liberal and sometimes conservative in their political reporting, were always probusiness and only too happy to run anti-union stories. The basic conservative argument used against the unions was that union members were lazy, greedy, and ultimately unpatriotic and that unions destroyed productivity and weakened the economy. The themes of this argument were echoed almost daily by the Reagan administration. Using double-standard logic and outright falsehoods, it gave the middle class all the misinformation needed to detest the unions.

One trick employed by the Corporate Feudalists then, and still used to this day, was intentionally exaggerating how much union workers were paid. Sometimes the numbers were made up and reported as facts. Other times the numbers were created by adding the wages of retired workers, current workers, and management, dividing the income by the number of workers, then claiming that figure as the average union wage. People paying attention to the mainstream news are constantly treated to stories about overpaid union workers. However, the numbers are never compared to what the owners and stockholders receive. That's because in the conservative United States created since the 1980s these groups are perceived differently. People at the top are honored for taking all they can, while middle-class workers are vilified when they fight for relative scraps.

To put things in perspective, it is informative to look at the incomes of corporate executives and workers in other countries in relation to the United States. In Japan, for example, senior executives receive an average of sixteen times more per hour than factory workers. If the average factory worker gets $10 an hour, the CEO receives $110 per hour. In Germany senior executives receive twenty times more per hour than factory workers, and in France the average CEO receives twenty-three times more. In all three of these examples, there is a comprehensible proportional relationship between labor's and management's compensation. In the conservative America created since the Reagan Revolution, however, CEOs may receive four hundred seventy-five times more per hour than the average factory worker, reflecting a lack of comprehensible proportional relationship between labor's and management's compensation. The US mainstream media as well as the conservative propaganda machine, including Foxaganda, maintain this double standard by not talking about it.

Forcing the US middle class to accept this glaringly inequitable situation might appear to be difficult. But using the motivators of fear, anger, and greed the Corporate Feudalists accomplished this task with relative ease. When Reagan took office, about 24 percent of the United States was made up of union households, affording conservatives a built-in "us versus them" situation. Because the plan for Corporate Feudalism involved claiming that conservatives were on the side of the little guy, it was easy to point out how union workers got more than nonunion workers. To exacerbate this disparity, stories were constantly fed to the media about seemingly ridiculous examples of union abuse, such as large union donations to political candidates or corruption of union officials. The debate changed from how the middle class should have good wages and quality of life to why union workers should not receive more than nonunion workers—the result of a classic "divide and conquer" strategy.

To instill even more anger and fear in the American public, each time a company moved overseas the unions were blamed. The elimination of tariffs or other global free trade initiatives was never mentioned, making it appear as though these moves were not the fault of greedy or unpatriotic owners who didn't care about US workers but of the selfish, greedy union workers themselves. Consequently, while the conservatives were dismantling the US industrial base and transferring the wealth from US workers to the Corporate Feudalists, they were able to blame union workers for these changes. The fear of job losses, combined with the daily dose of blame laid at the feet of the unions, created the perfect scenario to further weaken and destroy the unions. All the while, the real culprit—global free trade—was ignored or misunderstood.

Early on in his administration, Reagan's personal charisma was used to make union bashing fashionable. When the air traffic controllers went on strike in 1981, Reagan simply disbanded the entire union, making it clear that his conservative government had the power to destroy a union if it dared to demand safe working conditions or fair wages. Nonunion workers cheered Reagan's boldness, not realizing that it was their jobs and their children's that would be put in jeopardy as a result.

In just a few short years, middle-class workers went from admiring and emulating union workers to vilifying them. Reagan and the Corporate Feudalists had done their job well;

thirty years after Reagan began his assault on the unions the same arguments are still being used. When the US auto industry faced the possibility of collapse at the end of George W. Bush's administration, the unions were blamed. While we are continually fed exaggerated claims about union compensation, we are never provided with a comparison between union and management compensation. Does upper management make one thousand times more per hour? Ten thousand times more? We do not know. We are not supposed to.

How often do we hear about the fact that US middle-class workers cannot possibly compete financially with Chinese workers, who can survive on a few dollars a day? How often do we hear how the elimination of tariffs has made it impossible for the US middle class to survive? How often do we hear that the conservative policies promoted for the past thirty years have led directly to our current economic crisis? Never. But we hear a great deal about how much union workers are supposedly overpaid.

The conservatives' effort to weaken the unions has successfully jump-started a race to the bottom. US workers may continue taking wage concessions as long as they can. But they will remain unable to stop the decline in wages until they are willing to live like Chinese workers, or other populations where the term "middle class" means something quite different from what it meant in the United States just thirty years ago.

If you happen to be someone at the very top who will become one of the new feudal lords, this all looks good. The elimination of the unions has made it much more feasible for you to take your rightful place not just as an economic leader but also as a ruler. The life of the US middle class has just about run its course. It is almost time for you to start dictating your terms and stop sharing the wealth. Soon you will be able to decide who eats and who starves, the way it was before unions were introduced—and the way some people believe it should be again.

Did you think of a better way to weaken or discredit unions than the strategies used by the Corporate Feudalists? Or did you conclude that the plan they implemented was the best one available?

CHAPTER 9

Step Four: The Magic of Tax Cuts

W hat would you do? Your goal for this step is to convince people that taxes are always bad and should be opposed as a matter of principle. How would you sell this idea to the American public?

Tax cuts were one of the staples of the Reagan Revolution, and it would be hard for anyone looking back at the last thirty years of US history to deny the success of this part of the plan for Corporate Feudalism. Unlike the changes made to the mainstream media, which were implemented as secretly as possible, tax cuts were loudly proclaimed as one of the great principles of the new conservative revolution. It has become the mantra of Republicans to oppose taxes. Today, both Republicans and Democrats are largely defined by how many tax cuts they favor and how many taxes they oppose.

Thirty years ago, Reagan and the Republicans introduced a very simple concept to the American public to promote tax cuts. The Reagan administration claimed that the government had way more money than it needed and that because of all the waste in government the administration could cut taxes without affecting services the middle class wanted and expected. It was basically the promise of something for nothing. In an institution the size of the US government, it was easy to find examples of waste to make the argument appear plausible. For example, there were welfare mothers driving Cadillacs and Pentagon hammers that cost $300.

At the same time the promise of tax cuts was being sold, Reagan went out of his way to attack the federal government and its workers as the enemy of the people, wasting their hard-earned taxpayer dollars for foolish and fraudulent reasons. The classic one-liner Reagan employed to make this point was his "nine scariest words" in the English language: "I'm from the government and I'm here to help." Who wouldn't want to cut taxes when people were continually told about how the bureaucrats intentionally squandered taxpayer money and that all of the same government services would remain after the taxes were cut?

However, contrary to this promise, the people who created the plan for Corporate Feudalism realized that, over time, services the public deemed essential would have to be cut, although they knew that many of these changes would happen slowly so that people would not easily realize what was happening to the services they depended upon and, more importantly, would not connect the loss of services to tax cuts. This strategy parallels the anecdote of the boiling frog. The premise of the story is that if a frog is placed in boiling water it will jump out to escape harm. If, however, the frog is placed in tepid water, which is slowly heated to the boiling point, the frog won't realize the danger until it is too late. The Reagan administration hoped that this same lack of realization would hold true with taxpayers if public services were cut incrementally over time. They correctly assumed that the effect of their tax cuts would go unnoticed until it was too late. One significant way conservatives hid the effects of their tax cuts was by eliminating money to repair and replace vital infrastructure. This was the equivalent of a person saving money by not changing the oil in a car or by ignoring a leaky roof. The individual might have money in their pocket in the short term, but when their roof collapsed or their engine needed to be replaced due to lack of maintenance the cost would be much greater, and they might not have the money to fix it at all.

Another key selling point of Reaganomics was the theory called trickle-down economics. According to this theory, cutting taxes on the wealthy would result in a rising tide of prosperity for all. The idea was that by putting more money in the hands of the leaders of industry, now called the job creators, more jobs would be created for the middle class and working poor. Even though some members of his own party originally decried this theory, Reagan and the Corporate Feudalists stuck with it throughout the past thirty years, and it is still a tenet of those who believe all tax cuts will result in prosperity for all Americans.

Focusing the American public's attention on tax cuts helped move the United States toward Corporate Feudalism in several ways. First, once the idea of "taxes are always bad" was accepted by the general public, the transfer of wealth from the middle class to the superrich could begin in earnest. Because taxes in general were now considered "bad" and, therefore, any tax cut was "good," even people living below the poverty line cheered when taxes on billionaires were reduced. This strategy worked in part because Republicans had convinced many people in the middle class that we all shared a common enemy in taxes and our government.

Second, focusing the American public's attention on tax cuts helped move the United States toward Corporate Feudalism by increasing the national debt. While the promise of the Reagan Revolution was to cut taxes and balance budgets, fulfillment of that promise looked very different. In fact, during its eight-year run the Reagan administration created the largest budget deficit and national debt in the history of the United States up to that point. Although the size of the deficit was reported, its connection to the conservative tax cut plan was rarely made. More importantly, the future elimination of services that would be required because of the ballooning federal budget deficit was never mentioned.

To the average person, budget deficits and increasing national debt might seem like a bad thing. But if you were part of a small group of people hoping to move the United States toward Corporate Feudalism, uncontrolled budget deficits and a rising national debt looked downright brilliant. For one thing, if your goal was to eliminate popular programs like health care, public education, and Social Security, you would need a reason, and a budget deficit would provide the rationale needed to cut services for the middle class. This would be especially true if you had already convinced the public that any politician who suggests an increase in taxes to pay for services needs to be removed from office. In addition, even bankrupting the US government would help lead the country away from middle-class democracy and toward feudalism. Once the country was bankrupt, the new feudal lords would have complete control over how things were done in the name of managing the economic crisis. This can be seen playing out today as conservatives insist on cutting popular middle-class programs because the "excessive national debt and budget deficit" makes it necessary.

While the conservatives continually claimed that they could cut taxes without eliminating services, what actually took place after their tax cuts were introduced included both the elimination of essential services and an exponential growth of the national debt. At first the effects of fewer government services were borne by the very poor and powerless, as cuts to welfare and mental health facilities were made almost immediately. During the 1980s, thousands of mentally ill patients were forced to leave federally funded mental institutions, often ending up homeless. In fact, there was an explosion in the number of homeless people in the United States that began during the Reagan administration. But these homeless people were basically invisible to members of the middle class, most of whom had not yet been affected by the cuts in services, and so most people never noticed.

The connection between the federal budget deficit and the tax cuts could be seen by anyone who was looking carefully almost as soon as the Reagan Revolution began, as could the need to eliminate services to pay for these tax cuts. Yet conservatives continued to claim that they were only cutting fat from the system. Now, thirty years later, cuts to services have reached across the board to all middle-class programs. The federal budget deficit is the largest in history, and the US infrastructure is crumbling in large part because of thirty years of deferred maintenance as a result of these tax cuts.

Yet to this day conservatives vilify as enemies of the people any politicians who suggest raising taxes on even the largest corporations or wealthiest billionaires. So the problems continue to multiply. Because a massive share of the tax cuts promoted and passed by conservatives since the Reagan Revolution have benefited the superrich, the tax burden has shifted to the middle class and the very poor. One result of this shifting tax burden is that the middle class now owns a much larger share of the ballooning national debt than they would have before the tax cutting began. It is like someone using your credit card for thirty years without your noticing or anyone telling you about it. When you finally do get the bill, you might go bankrupt, as many in the middle class have been forced to do today. But that has not silenced the conservatives, who still claim that tax cuts for the superrich somehow help the middle class.

It is hard to imagine a more successful strategy for convincing the US middle class that all taxes are bad and all tax cuts are good than the one used by the Corporate Feudalists for the past thirty years. Did you perhaps find a better plan? Or would you agree that their plan has worked nearly perfectly to convince a large segment of the middle class that even as their services are cut and the nation's infrastructure collapses, tax cuts are invariably good and taxes are bad?

CHAPTER 10

Step Five: Teaching People to Hate Their Government

What would you do? Your goal for this step is to figure out how to teach the middle class to hate their own government using a strategy that takes into consideration the political climate of the United States of thirty years ago.

Teaching the middle class to hate their government was an essential part of the plan to implement Corporate Feudalism. A middle class cannot exist without a strong government. This is because only a government has the power to stand up to the giant corporations of today's world, or the powerful individuals and private armies of earlier times. It is the government that enforces the laws to protect the middle class from those who would like to become their economic rulers. That is why prior to the Industrial Revolution and the creation of the middle class all economies were run according to some version of the feudal system. If you want to put an end to the middle class and replace it with a feudal republic, you would need to change people's perception of their government.

Obviously a government does not have to be on the side of its people, as can be seen by the existence of countless dictatorships and oligarchies throughout the world. Even the corporatocracy that currently exists in the United States falls far short of being on the side of its middle class. But US history shows that a government committed to serving its citizens can, in fact, help create and maintain a healthy middle class even in the face of powerful corporations whose only interest is maximizing their own power and profits.

It is like the story in old westerns of a big bad landowner who takes what he wants when he wants it, ruthlessly terrorizing a town without a strong sheriff. Any individual who tries to stop the landowner is beaten into submission or killed. The situation continues until the town finds a strong enough sheriff to regain control over the landowner and his gang. This is the Old West version of the feudal system. In westerns, the feudal lord comes first and the sheriff comes later. But in the United States of thirty years ago, the government was the strong sheriff keeping the late-twentieth-century feudal lords from taking what they wanted. As long as the government was supported by its citizens—particularly its middle class—no one could ride into town and steal what belonged to the people. But if the government were weakened or destroyed, a different situation would arise. The intent of the plan for Corporate Feudalism was to convince the middle class to fire their sheriff. And that's just what happened.

Thirty years ago at the onset of the Reagan Revolution, the middle class basically appreciated and respected their government and believed that living in the United States was good for the middle class. They took their status for granted. The connection between what was good about the United States and its government was clear to the American public. For the most part, people believed the government was on their side and largely responsible for the high standard of living they enjoyed. Their government built the roads that made transportation easy. Their government made the laws and regulations that kept US workers safe at their jobs. Their government ensured that their food was safe. The labor strife that had empowered the middle class was now decades old, and the Vietnam War had ended, although not well. In many ways the United States of thirty years ago was a happy place, and most people understood their government's role in keeping it that way. While there were problems, including the energy crisis, they seemed manageable. Not everyone was happy with everything the government did, of course, but there was general agreement that the US government was the best government anywhere.

Then the US government found itself in the crosshairs of the brand-new Reagan Revolution with no way to understand why it was under attack and no way to defend itself. For thirty years, it took blow after blow. Now, while still standing, that government is very different from what it was when Reagan took office. It is much weaker, no longer able to offer the protections or provide the services the middle class took for granted thirty years ago—the same kinds of services that many European democracies have continued to provide for their citizens during the period of US economic and social decline. And in its weakened state the US government has lost the support of the very citizens who depended on it the most, the middle class.

How did this happen? When Ronald Reagan got to Washington, he set out to convince the middle class that their government was their enemy, using his considerable powers of persuasion. The basic message of Reagan and the conservatives was that everyone would be better off if the federal government just disappeared. They were smart enough not to say this directly, however. Instead, they just landed one body blow after another without openly expressing their desire to destroy the government.

For example, Reagan attacked government workers, contending they were lazy, wasted taxpayer money, and involved themselves in issues they knew nothing about, like regulating large businesses and corporations. Within the first few years of Reagan's election, the morale of the federal workforce plummeted as these employees saw their image shift from being considered public servants trying to make life in the United States better for everyone to being seen as lazy, despised bureaucrats wasting taxpayer money. Far from being a place where committed public servants worked to help the public, Washington, DC, became known as the place where crooks, thieves, and lazy workers stole taxpayer money for foolish purposes or their own personal benefit.

While federal workers had unions to protect their jobs, they did not have high-priced lobbyists and media consultants to safeguard their image. The unions representing federal workers came under the same harsh attack as the workers themselves, but the attacks went largely unanswered. The nation's first movie star president had intentionally created this negative image of government workers, and he was convincing.

Following Reagan, other conservatives continued to lead the charge against the government, often using the same language the Reagan administration had employed. Few found language more effective than the Reagan one-liner "I'm from the government and I'm here to help," but they didn't need to. The leap from John F. Kennedy's "Ask not what your country can do for you, but what you can do for your country" to Reagan's cynical and supposedly frightening "I'm from the government and I'm here to help" had been successfully made.

In addition to waging a full-scale campaign against the government and its employees, the Reagan administration also implemented another practice that was equally destructive to the image of government—filling government positions with people who hated government, a practice that continues to this day. For those seeking to change the United States from a middle-class democracy to a corporate feudal republic, there are three major advantages to this practice. First, you give government jobs to your conservative friends and cronies. Second, you keep dedicated public servants who want to see government succeed out of government. Third, and most importantly, you have a cadre of conservative ideologues working inside the government to sabotage and destroy the government at every turn.

The advantages for conservatives of sabotaging and destroying the government are almost limitless. Looking at a few examples from George W. Bush's administration shows why. Thirty years ago the Consumer Product Safety Commission (CPSC), a government agency committed to protecting the public by monitoring the safety of toys and other products, made a positive difference in people's lives. However, during George W. Bush's administration conservatives who filled many of the civil service positions and all of the politically appointed slots did not believe the government should be in the business of helping to protect the public, and they did everything in their power to avoid carrying out their responsibilities. When Congress tried to give the CPSC more money to do a better job of regulating products imported from China, for example, the Bush-appointed agency head refused. She said they had plenty of money to do their job, although in reality they weren't doing their job at all. Then reports started coming in about unsafe toys originating in China. People were outraged, as they should have been, and blamed the government. By failing to do their jobs, the conservatives were encouraging people to give up on their own government, which was exactly what conservatives wanted.

Thirty years ago, in an effort to make their point, conservatives often exaggerated the examples of government corruption and waste, but during George W. Bush's administration scandals involving everything from toys to military contracting became the norm. And who were the perpetrators of most of these crimes against the United States and its taxpayers? They were government-hating conservatives working inside the government, placed there for this very reason. Each time one of these conservatives was caught in another scandal, the American public's view of government deteriorated a little more. If you believe in a government that helps its citizens, this seems bad. But if you believe that the best government is no government this seems great, so the people who wanted to establish Corporate Feudalism couldn't have been happier.

That was the plan used by Corporate Feudalists to convince millions of middle-class people to hate their own government. Did you think of a more effective way to accomplish this goal? Or do you believe the plan that was used was the most effective one available?

CHAPTER 11

Step Six: Privatizing ("Piratizing") Government

What would you do? Your goal for this step is to convince middle-class citizens that turning their taxpayer money over to private corporations is a better idea than letting the government itself spend the money for services. What means would you employ to accomplish this task?

Before the Reagan Revolution, the federal government provided services that helped the general public, including building and maintaining roads, protecting the environment, and Medicare and other health services. Middle-class citizens knew that their taxes were being used to improve their daily lives and society as a whole.

But reducing the size of the federal government was an important part of the program to eliminate the US middle class and institute Corporate Feudalism, and privatizing government services was a way to help achieve this. Privatization of government services was one of the Reagan Revolution's easiest goals to achieve. The basic idea was that many of the services the government was performing could and should be done by the private sector instead because government was inherently inefficient and wasteful, while private industry and corporations were inherently efficient and prudent. In many ways, the privatization argument became another way to reinforce the attacks conservatives were making on unions and on the government itself.

According to conservatives, because the private sector could provide the same services as the government but more efficiently and for less money, it would save the taxpayers millions or even billions of dollars. Since this argument seemed appealing with minimal controversy, the Reagan administration started turning public services over to the private sector. Commissions were established with the sole purpose of identifying government services that could be privatized. An entire industry developed with a financial stake in promoting the idea that government workers were inefficient, while the private sector was saving taxpayer dollars at every turn. Subsequently, the privatization of government services led to private consultants and contractors receiving millions of taxpayer dollars with little or no government oversight. As a result, billions of dollars were transferred directly from taxpayers to privately held corporations. Over the past thirty years, handing US taxpayer dollars over to private corporations has become a commonplace and mostly unquestioned practice. Today, there is probably no function performed by government workers and paid for by taxpayer dollars that is not performed somewhere else by private contractors using US taxpayer money.

Like so many other claims made by the conservatives, privatizing government was never vetted. Reagan's claim that privatization would save taxpayers money and his salesmanship ability, as well as the difficulty involved in tracing how taxpayer money was being spent by private consultants and contractors, resulted in this policy just being accepted.

However, there is little to no oversight of how all this taxpayer money has been spent or whether it has saved the taxpayers any money or actually costs taxpayers much more. What is known is troubling, to say the least. Many of the private recipients of this taxpayer money are also in the business of lobbying the government that feeds them and giving large campaign contributions to their friends on Capitol Hill. In addition, much of this taxpayer money goes directly into the pockets of the millionaire owners of large corporations and not to the people actually doing the work.

Privatization, or more aptly "piratization," has played a major role in promoting several of the other steps to Corporate Feudalism. First, since the number of functions performed by a government as large as that of the United States is massive, when these functions become privatized the size of the union workforce is diminished. Thus privatization fits perfectly with the goal of destroying unions, an essential component of the plan for Corporate Feudalism. In many ways, federal government positions are one example of what good middle-class jobs should look like. Protected by unions from the abuses of unscrupulous employers, government jobs are an important element of economies around the world. Such jobs pay a living wage, provide pensions, and are secure. Not only can individual workers depend on them, but so can the various businesses supported by these workers. By contrast, privatized taxpayer-funded jobs are often temporary, as they may be up for a new contract each year, and they offer no union protections against incompetent or unscrupulous employers. Privatized jobs may pay more or they may pay less than a corresponding government job, but they are always less secure. By eliminating stability, an important part of what makes up a middle-class job is lost.

Second, because the argument of privatization is based on the idea that government bureaucracies are wasteful, it helps teach people to hate their government, another essential component of the plan for Corporate Feudalism. Thus a further role of privatization of government services has been providing a platform for conservative propaganda. For thirty years, the public has been exposed to the same conservative messages: government workers are bad, corporate business is good; unions are bad, corporations are good; government workers are inefficient, private corporations are efficient. Thirty years of repetition is enough to sway millions of people, especially when voices providing a different side to the story are drowned out.

Third, because contracts for privatized work can be awarded to private companies at any time and any place, oversight becomes next to impossible and lack of accountability can be exploited, yet another essential component of the plan for Corporate Feudalism. There is no way to prove whether privatization costs more or less than the same services provided by government workers. What is known is that with government jobs the money goes directly to middle-class workers, while with privatized jobs a few well-connected millionaires and billionaires are taking a cut from taxpayer money. No doubt, often these privatized contracts are little more than transfer payments from US taxpayers directly to the Corporate Feudalists themselves.

Although exploiting lack of accountability enriches the people who plan to become the feudal lords of the future, it can also be used to hide the true costs of unpopular or illegal actions. While it is relatively easy to identify how much the US military or the State Department is spending on a particular project, such as the second Iraq War, private contractors are much less transparent with their financial data. The finances of private companies may be mixed together in such a way that it is impossible for anyone but the company executives to trace and comprehend. Certain contracts, like the lucrative no-bid ones given to Halliburton, may be impossible to track, and many other private businesses have multiuse contracts as well, so while some money may be spent on a specified project, other amounts may be spent in totally different areas. This lack of transparency keeps the public and even Congress in the dark about how much taxpayer money is being spent in a particular area.

Lack of accountability surrounding privatization can also mask illegal actions. For example, during the Contra War against Nicaragua Congress explicitly forbade the Reagan administration from continuing to wage this war. The Reaganites ignored Congress, however, and continued the war against Nicaragua by other means, including selling weapons to our supposed enemies in Iran and using the money for the Contras in Nicaragua. CIA resources were used illegally, and some of our allies were pressured to provide money for this operation. These illegal actions were eventually exposed, and several Reagan administration officials were convicted of crimes associated with this activity. However, all these illegal activities took place prior to the days of rampant privatization. Today, with so much taxpayer money flowing to private companies for government business, it would be possible to mount an entire terrorist war against a small country like Nicaragua completely off the books.

Another example of how the lack of accountability due to privatization can hide illegal actions is the torture of prisoners at Abu Ghraib in Iraq during George W. Bush's administration. Some of the mysterious individuals who brought shame to the United States through their actions at Abu Ghraib were private contractors. Several were present at illegal interrogations and may have personally participated in the torture that took place. They had the authority to tell military personnel what to do and were definitely involved in promoting the torture. Yet no one knows who these people were or for whom they worked. Even today, the amount of taxpayer dollars paid to contractors connected with this torture remains unknown.

Still another example of how lack of accountability surrounding privatization can potentially mask illegal actions is surveillance. For example, we know that private phone companies were ordered to provide specific information to George W. Bush's administration. But we do not know how much surveillance was done and who was spied on, because this work was carried out by private businesses that are not accountable to the public. When these problems are multiplied by the billions of taxpayer dollars given to private companies each year, it becomes apparent that the potential for abuse is staggering. So while it is impossible to compare the exact dollar-for-dollar use of taxpayer money between government workers on the one hand and privatized government contractors on the other, some things are apparent. With government workers, it is easy to examine which services are being provided at what cost to taxpayers. With private contractors, however, it is nearly impossible. With government employees it is very difficult to promote and very easy to detect any large-scale illegal activities such as torture and domestic surveillance. With private contractors, on the other hand, masking illegal activities is simply a matter of hiring companies willing and able to carry out the administration's desires.

A further important difference between services provided by government employees and those provided by private contractors is that with government employees all of the taxpayer dollars go directly to middle-class workers. There are obvious differences in pay between people at the top and lower levels of government employment, but all such employees lie somewhere on the scale of the middle-class workforce. However, the opposite is true with privatized government services, in which huge chunks of taxpayer dollars go directly to the millionaire and billionaire owners of the private corporations that have contracts for these services. One of two things must be happening, or perhaps both together: either the workers providing the privatized government services are being paid less than a comparable government employee or the government is paying more to the private contractor for the same service. In either case, these privatized government services have made the rich richer, transferring taxpayer dollars directly from middle-class citizens into the bank accounts of the wealthy.

For thirty years, this sleight of hand—the whole corrupt system of privatized government services—continued, for the most part, undetected, but now it is exposed for anyone who wants to see it. One glaring example that has opened some eyes to the rip-off that we call privatized government services involves the Iraq War. First, we learned about the multimillion-dollar no-bid contracts given to oil services company Halliburton by its former CEO, Vice President Dick Cheney, for all sorts of operations in Iraq. Then we were told how millions of these taxpayer dollars disappeared without delivery of the contracted services. We learned from whistle-blowers that Halliburton received premium prices and then intentionally provided inferior products to our troops in the field. We discovered how Halliburton executives lived like royalty in luxury hotels, all paid for by US taxpayers. We also found out that taxpayer money was given to private companies to train and deploy mercenaries in Iraq. These mercenaries, who did not need to follow the rules of conduct that our troops were required to adhere to, ultimately were responsible for some of the worst abuses in Iraq, violations that gave our country and military a bad name around the world. All the while, the mercenaries were being paid three to four times more than our own military personnel, often for the same work.

Armed soldiers answering to private corporations, acting under different rules than the military of the United States, and fighting side by side with our own military while being paid so much more is not a great morale booster for our military. The percentage of taxpayer money turned over to private security contractors like Blackwater—renamed Xe and then renamed Academi—that goes to the owners and executives before they hand out their mercenary contracts remains unknown. They are private businesses, after all, and even though it is US taxpayer money we do not have the right to know. This is one clear example of how the United States is not saving money by hiring private companies to run aspects of our wars.

Like other government workers, our soldiers are part of America's middle class. The owners and executives of companies like Halliburton and Blackwater, on the other hand, are part of the plan for Corporate Feudalism. The multimillion-dollar transfer payments of taxpayer money to private corporations to fight unnecessary wars helps promote feudalism, but it certainly does not help the US middle class.

Handing US taxpayer dollars over to private corporations has become a commonplace and mostly unquestioned practice over the past thirty years. Did you think of a better way to convince the public of the merits of privatizing government services than the arguments used by the Corporate Feudalists? Or did you find that their plan was the best way to accomplish this goal?

CHAPTER 12

Step Seven: Deregulating American Business

What would you do? Your goal for this step is to convince middle-class citizens that they will benefit by deregulating US corporations. How would you convince the American electorate that deregulation of large corporations can work to their advantage?

As with step four, which touted the magic of tax cuts, deregulating American business was another part of the plan for Corporate Feudalism that was openly advocated. The theory put forth by conservatives was that government regulation of businesses was bad and that the private sector could regulate itself much more efficiently and economically. If businesses could regulate themselves more efficiently and economically, why should taxpayers pay to do it through government regulation? According to this theory, government regulation was yet another example of a bloated government wasting taxpayer money on something unnecessary, and deregulating businesses could eliminate thousands of unnecessary government workers (called "bureaucrats" by the conservatives) and save millions of dollars in taxpayer money at the same time. In addition, conservatives claimed that because businesses would then spend less money complying with needless government regulations they could spend more on hiring workers, making the US economy that much more healthy and vibrant.

Propelled by this argument, removing government regulations from businesses became a major goal of the Reagan Revolution and continues to this day to be a rallying cry for conservatives. Like other parts of the plan for Corporate Feudalism, deregulation was incredibly effective in helping eliminate the middle class and move the country toward Corporate Feudalism. Once again, the people were promised they would get something for nothing.

Through yet another brilliant sales job, the Reagan administration started deregulating everything from media ownership to environmental protection policies. Frequently the potential damage to the middle class was not apparent initially because there were no immediate noticeable consequences. If the conservatives eliminated an air quality regulation, for example, it would take years for the effects to be seen, and by then no one would think to blame the deregulation that had taken place so long before.

In some instances, deregulation of American businesses was felt rather quickly, however. The deregulation of the savings and loan and financial industries is one example. Deregulation of these industries meant there was more quick money to be made by speculators and traders. As a result, many new industries based on arbitrage and hostile takeovers were created, and a boomtown mentality invaded the financial markets. In addition to deregulation, conservatives in the Reagan administration began to ignore regulations they could not eliminate, leaving even the regulated industries free to do as they pleased. In the financial markets, this meant ignoring rules put in place to protect taxpayers and small investors.

Many of the gains seen in the financial sector during the Reagan administration resulted from the destruction and cannibalization of healthy US corporations. The fear of hostile takeovers forced even financially sound corporations into a frenzy of cost-cutting measures that included the elimination of middle-class jobs. These strategies did not always help the companies in question, and they resulted in fewer jobs for average Americans. At the same time that large numbers of jobs were being cut at the beginning of what became known as the "downsizing" movement, people at the top were making sums that just a few years earlier would have been considered immoral fortunes. Once again, the Corporate Feudalists were able to implement a policy that contributed directly to the transfer of wealth from the middle class to the superrich.

In addition to deregulating American businesses, all regulations that penalized US companies for moving overseas and importing their products back to the United States were also attacked. Conservatives derisively labeled these regulations "protectionist," claiming that US workers and the US economy would be much better off with free trade as opposed to protected trade. Again, no proof was offered that such an approach would work, but the unyielding conservative promise of a better economy and more better-paying jobs for Americans was enough to sway a large segment of the middle class who were already in fear of losing their jobs. The elimination of tariffs protecting US workers was the beginning of the global free trade hoax, a part of the plan for Corporate Feudalism addressed in the next chapter.

Because the effects of global free trade and deregulation often take years to recognize, it is difficult to determine just how much long-term damage deregulating American businesses and overseas trading has done to the US economy and middle class. However, some short-term effects have already damaged US corporations and negatively impacted US taxpayers. The stock market crash of 1987, for example, cost stockholders millions of dollars, and the jobs lost when deregulated speculators started buying and tearing apart healthy US corporations for short-term gain never returned.

The savings and loan crash of the mid-1980s is evidence of yet another disaster for US taxpayers caused by deregulation. Once the Reagan administration deregulated the savings and loan industry, speculators easily moved into that sector of the American economy. Instead of the self-regulation promised by conservatives, we saw greed and theft that would make a drunken sailor blush. When the excesses of the savings and loan industry reached a tipping point, not even the help of several insider congressmen—including John McCain—could save it. Instead, US taxpayers were forced to spend $125 million to bail out the savings and loans once this deregulated industry failed. The $125 million bailout held the record as the nation's largest but pales in comparison to the Bush banking and financial bailout of 2008.

Did this financial disaster caused by deregulation slow conservatives down in their efforts to promote more deregulation? Did these failures at least force conservatives to view deregulation as a mixed bag? Of course not. Today, thirty years after Ronald Reagan first implemented deregulation, the granddaddy of deregulation failures—the results of deregulation of the banking and mortgage industries—is staring us in the face. During George W. Bush's second term in office, conservatives were able to almost completely deregulate the banking and mortgage industries. In those few instances where they were unable to deregulate parts of the industry, they simply filled the regulatory agencies controlling these parts with people who had no intention of enforcing the existing regulations. What followed was precisely what critics of deregulation had claimed would happen, and the opposite of what conservatives had promised.

Once deregulation had impacted the banking and mortgage industries, it was every crook for him- or herself. Every imaginable con was used to take advantage of or defraud unsuspecting consumers. Loans were intentionally made to borrowers who could not afford them over the long term. Often mortgage brokers would purposely lie about the products they were selling, and people with affordable, fixed-rate mortgages were convinced to change to adjustable-rate mortgages lenders knew they could not pay. In many of these deals, the lender ended up with both the borrower's house and property, and the middle-class borrower ended up in foreclosure. With little or no regulation and conservatives in government looking the other way, the mortgage scam that led to the housing crisis beginning in 2008 transferred vast amounts of wealth from the middle class to the superrich. Yet conservative claims that deregulation is always a good thing continue, as do the disasters caused by deregulation. It is interesting to note that while these financial disasters have cost small investors and taxpayers billions upon billions in lost funds, they have continued to accelerate the flow of money from the middle class to the superrich. Perhaps this is why conservatives are so willing to ignore the downside of deregulation.

After thirty years of believing the false promises of conservatives, with the onset of the housing crisis many middle-class people began realizing that they are vulnerable and now wonder what went wrong. They followed all the rules, they worked hard, and now they are losing their jobs and their homes. But they haven't figured out why, and conservatives are doing everything in their power to make sure they don't. Connecting the mortgage and banking collapse to deregulation is one small step in that process.

While conservative Republicans continue to make daily calls for deregulation of private business, the amount of deregulation that has already taken place is staggering. Did you come up with a better plan than the one discussed here to convince the American public that deregulation is a good idea? Or do you believe that the plan they used was the most effective one?

CHAPTER 13

Step Eight: The Global Free Trade Hoax

W hat would you do? Your goal for this step is to create a strategy that convinces a vibrant US middle class of thirty years ago that it is possible to compete with Third World laborers willing to work for three dollars a day and that global free trade will open foreign markets to US-made goods, preserving and creating American jobs.

While all fifteen steps to Corporate Feudalism were necessary to eliminate the middle class, some steps were more important than others, and initiating global free trade was among them. What was the promise of global free trade and how was the middle class convinced to accept it?

The idea of global free trade is simple enough—a world governed by unregulated capitalism, where goods and services move freely regardless of international boundaries. According to its proponents, its advantage is maximum efficiency, which, in turn, leads to maximum prosperity for the countries that participate in this system. The proponents of global free trade promised that it would create millions of jobs in the United States by opening up new markets for US products all over the world. It was going to be the engine that drove our economy to future prosperity.

To be persuaded by the promise of global free trade, you have to accept several free-market assumptions. First, you have to believe that unregulated capitalism is the best economic system. Second, you have to trust that corporations will serve the public interest and regulate themselves when necessary if government and unions can be controlled or, better yet, eliminated from the corporate process. Finally, you have to assume that maximizing corporate profits is always the best economic policy. In addition to buying into these free-market assumptions, you must also accept the idea that competition is beneficial and that protectionism is evil, as well as embrace the Reagan 1980s mantra "Greed is good." In the eyes of Corporate Feudalists, competition was the most significant component of an economy capable of making us stronger and better able to compete in the global marketplace. Any time a business failed in the United States, it was seen as a result of its lack of competitiveness. Sometimes businesses had to relocate overseas to be more competitive, but that was okay because being competitive was the ultimate goal.

The opposite of competition was protectionism. It was claimed that everything great and wholesome about competition could be destroyed by protectionist policies. Protectionism would weaken the US economy by making us less competitive. More importantly, we couldn't have global free trade if our country was protecting its own workers. Anything even remotely aimed at protecting US workers or jobs was considered anticompetitive and unacceptable, and anyone promoting such ideas was accused of wanting to destroy the US economy. Not surprisingly, looking at the preconditions for accepting global free trade we find the foundations of the Republican economic plan since the Reagan Revolution. The promise of benefits from global free trade was accepted and reported as fact by the mainstream media, convincing a large segment of the US middle class to believe in it. Voices crying in the wilderness, including US labor unions and progressive Democrats, were all but drowned out by the enthusiasm created by the pie-in-the-sky promise of the benefits of global free trade.

Of the fifteen steps to Corporate Feudalism, global free trade should have been one of the easiest to detect as threatening to the interests of the US middle class. Even as it was being introduced during the Reagan Revolution, many people, particularly Democrats and unions, pointed out that we would lose jobs and even sovereignty as a result, but the proponents of global free trade kept pitching the same ideas, and they still do. Then, when financially successful US corporations started moving their manufacturing overseas to maximize profits, everyone should have been able to see why global free trade would not work for the US middle class. Year after year, global free trade resulted in more and more components of America's manufacturing base being sent overseas. Global free trade became the false promise that bled the country dry and the workhorse making it next to impossible for this country to return to middle-class democracy after realizing what had been done to us by the Corporate Feudalists.

The promise of global free trade was nothing more than a smokescreen to relocate the manufacturing sector from the United States to countries with less expensive labor markets. The idea that the US middle class of thirty years ago, twenty years ago, ten years ago, or even today could compete with people willing to work for a few dollars a week is ridiculous. By eliminating the manufacturing sector in the United States, the Corporate Feudalists eliminated the backbone of the US middle class. The fine balance that had been created between owners who needed workers and workers who needed jobs in the United States has been destroyed in the name of global free trade.

If more Americans had considered the impact of competing with laborers willing to work for incomprehensibly low wages, perhaps NAFTA and other free trade agreements would not have gone through. But instead, American workers were mesmerized into believing that global free trade would increase job security by opening new markets to their products.

In retrospect, the problems of global free trade seem so obvious that it is hard to imagine how anyone could have believed that a US middle-class worker with a house, one or even two cars, time for recreation, and the ability to send their children to college could compete with a worker willing to work for something like three dollars a day in a Third World country. It is not even a close call. When so much emphasis was placed on scrutinizing how much union workers were paid while completely ignoring how much owners, stockholders, and administrators received, middle-class citizens should have been suspicious. But the strong motivators of fear, anger, and greed were used to keep different parts of the middle class so fearful, angry, and separated from one another that the actions of the soon-to-be feudal lords went almost completely unexamined. United States citizens had a choice; we could have managed our resources and protected our middle-class way of life. Instead, we opened ourselves up to the whims of global free trade.

During the Industrial Revolution, the titans of manufacturing did not willingly give up their power or voluntarily share their wealth. They were forced into sharing their wealth through necessity, and this necessity resulted in the US middle class. Today, however, it looks like the middle class was a temporary necessity lasting only until those at the top could figure out how to eliminate it and return to a more feudal system of economic control.

More foundations of the US middle class have now been eliminated. Employees in the United States are willing to work for less and less in hopes of feeding their families. It is as if the US middle class were a ghost or a shadow—you imagine it is there because you are used to seeing it, but you can't quite catch it anymore. Although there are still people who live off the wealth generated by the middle class from previous generations, and there are individuals who fight hard to retain their middle-class lifestyle, these stances may only be holding back the tide.

If the manufacturing base had not been moved overseas, it would still be possible to revive the US middle class. But how can you stimulate an economy based on nothing more than consuming products that are produced somewhere else? For the past thirty years, we have lived off the productivity generated by the middle class before the plan for Corporate Feudalism was introduced. Now the US Treasury is empty, and the manufacturing base that created our wealth is gone. The middle class is stuck fighting over crumbs. The simple fact is that global free trade and the rest of the plan for Corporate Feudalism have already destroyed much of our middle-class economy.

After years of evidence proving that global free trade results in the elimination of American jobs, new free trade agreements are still being passed and many people still believe that global free trade is good for the middle class. Did you think of a better plan for selling global free trade to the American public than the one used by the Corporate Feudalists? Or did you find that their plan worked as well as any other might have?

CHAPTER 14

Step Nine: Destroying Public Education

What would you do? Your goal for this step is to devise a strategy to convince middle-class citizens that they don't want to support public education. This may look easy now, but remember, you need to go back thirty years to the time when public education was quite popular.

There were several reasons why destroying public education was critical to promoting Corporate Feudalism in the United States. For one thing, in the conservatives' view the only legitimate place for government spending was national defense and law and order. Public education cost a lot of money, and conservatives were philosophically opposed to it.

But simple conservative philosophy wasn't the only reason that destroying public education was so critical to promoting Corporate Feudalism. When this plan was introduced thirty years ago, the new feudal lords-in-waiting could see that their intent to send manufacturing jobs overseas would lead to a need for fewer educated workers, which would be further reduced with the introduction of computers and robotics. Perhaps most importantly, conservatives understood that a well-educated population would be much harder to control in their feudal republic.

Basically, conservatives wanted to create a compliant population that would do whatever they were told. The less people knew about the history of the middle class, the better. The less they knew about the rest of the world, the better. If US middle-class citizens could be taught to recite a few facts versus think for themselves, it would be perfect. A poorly educated public is easily manipulated, which, after all, was the goal of the plan for Corporate Feudalism, so they would accept and even support the elimination of the middle class.

By comparison, let's look at the role education plays in France, which offers all its citizens a high level of education. When the French government tries to promote policies that its middle- or even lower-class workers oppose, the workers put a quick stop to it. Organized farmers and truck drivers have shut the country down. The basic truth is this: if a group of powerful people tried to turn France into a feudal republic, they would have to use military force to accomplish their task since the public is too well educated to allow this to occur without a fight.

The same was true in the United States of thirty years ago. Today, however, a large segment of the population has been sufficiently "dumbed down" to accept anything they are told. This dumbing down is a direct result of the conservatives' attack on public education, working alongside the other steps discussed in this book, notably the phony media that were created over the past thirty years and the conning of the Evangelical Church discussed in chapter 16. Some of the dumbing down is also a result of middle-class citizens being so stressed by the demands and difficulties of everyday life that they have little time to think about much more than eating, working, and paying the bills.

The question is how did a group of conservatives claiming that public education was one of their main priorities manage to do so much harm to this educational system in only thirty years? While some parts of the plan for Corporate Feudalism were straightforward and easy, such as rallying the American public to oppose taxes and government regulation, it would have been next to impossible to gain support for destroying public education. Because the creators of plan for Corporate Feudalism knew this, instead of trying to convince people of the unthinkable they simply used a different strategy. Unlike at an earlier time, when conservatives had tried to win arguments based on their validity but failed, they realized that the only way to gain support for more radical policies was to lie, claiming they supported the opposite of what they did or telling the public whatever they wanted to hear. This strategy seemed perfectly suited to destroying education.

Consequently, starting with the Reagan administration, conservatives loudly proclaimed that they supported public education. Sometimes they asserted that public education was a priority for them. Because public education was exactly what the middle class wanted, they embraced this view. Then, in the name of supporting public education, the conservatives launched a major assault on every element that comprised this system, and in so doing triggered an adversarial relationship between parents, communities, and schools. This attack also helped conservatives keep the discussion away from making schools a budgetary priority.

Because conservatives forcefully claimed they were advocates of improving public education, no one noticed their tactics for destroying public education. They first began to destroy public education by attacking the teachers. Claiming that some teachers were lazy and others were even worse, Reagan and his cohorts declared that the public schools were full of liberal teachers trying to propagandize children. Major attacks were also mounted against teachers' unions. As we have already seen, anti-union attacks were another part of the plan for Corporate Feudalism, but the attacks directed at school unions were part of the overall assault on public education as well.

An additional tactic used was to ensure that people taking over local school boards were sympathetic to the goals of the Corporate Feudalists. Like their counterparts in federal regulatory positions, these school board members simply followed the prescribed agenda, showing little regard for the laws in place or the good of the community. In effect, they worked from within to dismantle the very institution they claimed to be protecting and promoting.

Also, whenever the issue of school funding was discussed the conservatives argued that throwing money at the problem wouldn't work, while throwing money at issues important to the agenda of Corporate Feudalism—such as the military, private contractors doing government work, and foreign regimes—would be helpful. For instance, they sunk large sums of money into the Nicaraguan Contras, the Afghan Mujahedin, and other right-wing paramilitary organizations, as well as right-wing dictatorships, but increased spending for public education in the United States—one of their stated priorities—was disregarded.

The conservatives' strategy of claiming to support public education while undermining its very foundations continues to this day. The voucher programs they endorse, for instance, have two obvious benefits for conservatives. First, they transfer precious resources directly from public schools to private ones. Second, they create an image of public schools as inferior. As this image takes hold, it convinces more people who can afford private schools to leave the public school system.

George W. Bush administration's No Child Left Behind Act of 2001 has done a great deal to further erode, if not destroy, people's confidence in public education. For thirty years, conservatives had allowed the public education system to deteriorate by starving poor schools for funding while blaming teachers and school administrators for the resulting problems. The No Child Left Behind system was then introduced as a reform. Under this system, standardized tests were given to students at all of the nation's public schools, and those that could not get their students up to certain standards were punished.

Conservatives conned the Democrats into supporting the No Child Left Behind Act by promising to fully fund the initiative, which meant a large increase in funding for the public schools. However, the increased funding never occurred. Instead, all public school teachers had to focus on teaching a specific set of facts so that their students performed well on the standardized tests, and those who were unable or unwilling to do this were punished. Teaching to the tests left little or no time to instruct students in thinking creatively. In addition, no supplemental resources were given to poor school districts to help them catch up academically; instead, poor school districts were attacked and punished if their students were unable to attain parity with their wealthy counterparts. The punishment consisted of withholding funding from the poor schools and helping their best students transfer to different schools, which only caused the poorer schools to fall further behind.

But the No Child Left Behind Act is just the latest effort in the Corporate Feudalists' successful thirty-year plan to dumb down the American middle class. There are now several million Americans who believe anything they are told by conservative media and politicians. Many no longer believe scientists or academics, or people from other countries, regardless of their position, status, or experience. These millions of poorly educated people, who have been convinced to believe conservative politicians and right-wing media pundits, have become an army of ignorance. They never learned to think critically. If they are told that black is white and up is down by the people they have been taught to believe, they accept it. If they are told that sending their jobs overseas is good for them, they accept it. If they are told that their country has to go to war, they accept it. When they are told that billionaires need tax breaks, they accept that, too. It seems there is nothing they will not accept if it comes from right-wing conservative leaders.

This blind faith in conservative leaders is the result of many factors, all of which are part of their plan for Corporate Feudalism. But one of their most effective tools has been thirty years of attacks on public education in the name of improving this educational system. Regardless of claims to the contrary, there is no doubt that a large segment of the American public has been intentionally dumbed down in an effort to prepare them to accept anything they are told. While this dumbing down of the American electorate does not bode well for the US middle class, from the perspective of Corporate Feudalists it is success in the making.

Everywhere we look, support for public education has diminished significantly over the past thirty years. Do you think the plan used by the Corporate Feudalists for accomplishing this goal was brilliant? Or did you think of an even better way to drive a wedge between the American public and public education?

CHAPTER 15

Step Ten: Promoting Unnecessary Wars

What would you do? Your goal for this step is to create a strategy that will allow you to launch an unnecessary war without being arrested or impeached. How does your strategy compare to the one the conservatives used?

The Corporate Feudalists' use of wars to promote unrelated goals is part of a long tradition of conning the public into supporting policies they would otherwise oppose in a time of peace. Throughout history, governments have been fighting unnecessary wars to further unrelated goals or to "change the subject." If a country's leadership is challenged from within, a war with a traditional enemy can be counted on to rally support back home. In the case of the Corporate Feudalists, their goal was not to generate public support but to weaken the US economy and destroy the middle class.

The first unnecessary war initiated by the Corporate Feudalists was the Contra War in Nicaragua. Once the Reagan administration assumed power, one of its top priorities became overthrowing the new Nicaraguan government. There were ideological reasons for this decision. The conservatives controlling the White House had no intention of allowing a nonaligned independent democracy to survive in Central America. While this war did not involve US troops or massive amounts of money, it allowed the Corporate Feudalists to test their model for waging unnecessary wars that was later used in both the first and second wars against Iraq.

The background for the Contra War was this: Nicaragua had been controlled by US-supported dictators for many years. The wealth of that nation was divided between a small oligarchy in Nicaragua and US multinational corporations. In 1979, the Nicaraguan people successfully overthrew their dictator. The majority of the Nicaraguan people viewed the revolution against the Sandinistas much like US citizens viewed their revolution against Great Britain. As in the American Revolutionary War, however, there were loyalists in Nicaragua who supported the old leadership. The US corporations that had controlled Nicaragua and the rest of Central America for many decades were not happy with the prospect of an independent country replacing what had previously been a US-friendly dictatorship.

Therefore, Reagan and his administration focused their efforts on convincing the American people that Nicaragua was a communist dictatorship. The Corporate Feudalists' plan was to create a new reality out of thin air by fabricating the story of Nicaragua being a communist dictatorship. They simply stated that black was white and up was down, then sold their version of reality to the American people, initiating the Contra War in Nicaragua. They did this by funding a proxy army, using many of the top military commanders from the previous dictatorship, in order to overthrow the elected government of Nicaragua, resulting in a war waged against civilians. Roads were land mined and villages attacked. Teachers, doctors, nurses, and police were assassinated. All of these atrocities would have been accurately called terrorism by the Reagan administration had it not perpetrated the acts.

In addition, they had to force the media to cover the Contra War from the conservative perspective. They accomplished this by employing several strategies. First, they used the conservative media to tell their version of the story verbatim. Second, they used the bully pulpit of the White House to spread their version of reality to the real media. Lastly, reporters who did not toe the Reagan line were called "leftists" or "unpatriotic," and punished in various ways.

However, there was a problem with selling the conservative version of events in Nicaragua to the media and the public. For one thing, the rest of the free world had a very different view. The new Nicaraguan government had received awards from the United Nations for its great strides in health care and education for its people. Our European allies had certified the Nicaraguan elections as free and fair, and the large majority of Nicaraguans were clearly embracing their newfound freedom. Further, Nicaragua was so close to the United States geographically that reporters and even US citizens could easily travel there and back. This meant that conservatives had to try to force their view down the throats of reporters on the ground in Nicaragua, who could easily prove that what the conservatives were saying was false.

For example, when the Reagan administration started assembling its Contra army, the Nicaraguan government provided guns to their entire population so their citizens could defend themselves. So while US conservatives claimed that Nicaragua was a communist dictatorship, the Nicaraguan government was arming its entire population. And while reporters knew that dictatorships fear their own populations and never arm them, they were instructed to ignore what they saw and report what they were told by conservatives and the Reagan administration. Although the Reagan administration claimed to have classified intelligence that proved their claims, they refused to release it for "national security reasons."

Conservative politicians also convinced conservative church leaders to make their case against Nicaragua. Evangelical televangelists Jerry Falwell and Pat Robertson used their influential networks to claim that the Nicaraguan government was oppressing churchgoers in that country. But while these US churchmen-turned-politicians were repeating the Reagan administration's view, Nicaraguan churchgoers were telling reporters just the opposite.

Now America's first movie star president was leading the charge against the new Nicaraguan government, while the longtime church leadership in Nicaragua was telling sister churches in the United States that the US government, and Reagan in particular, was lying about their country. Some of these Nicaraguan church leaders were Evangelicals, such as Gustavo Parajon, a prominent figure in Nicaraguan Evangelical circles. Parajon had been traveling to the United States for many years as a member of the American Baptist

Foreign Mission Society, and he had had long and friendly ties with many US Baptist leaders and congregations well before the Nicaraguan revolution. When Reagan launched the Contra War, Parajon tried desperately to convince US Baptists and other Evangelicals that Reagan was not telling the truth about the new Nicaraguan government.

In some ways, it seems the choice for US Evangelical Christians would have been simple: should they believe a Hollywood movie star politician or should they believe an Evangelical leader, pastor, and Baptist missionary living in Nicaragua? Parajon asked US church leaders to come to Nicaragua and see for themselves what was happening. He said it was easy to demonstrate that the Reagan administration was not telling the truth about his country. Subsequently thousands of ordinary US Christians and Jews traveled to Nicaragua and came back to the United States convinced that the Reagan administration was lying about Nicaragua.

Despite evidence that the US government was lying about the reasons for its involvement in Nicaragua, most Evangelicals chose to put their faith in conservative politicians instead of Nicaraguan church leaders or the returning US Christians. With this, it became obvious how far the US Evangelical Church could be pushed by conservative politicians. Once this previously nonpolitical group of Evangelical Christians was hooked by conservatives, they were hooked for good—proving to the Corporate Feudalists that they could own the Evangelicals. If US Evangelicals remained committed to conservative US politicians even when they waged an unnecessary, unjust war against a Christian country like Nicaragua while other Christians were telling them the US government was lying, then these Evangelicals could be counted on to support any war, anywhere, especially a war against a non-Christian country.

Another important element of the conservatives' Contra War against Nicaragua was testing how far our government could push our allies to support us, or at least remain neutral when we engaged in unjust and unnecessary wars. Our Democratic allies knew that Nicaragua was not a totalitarian dictatorship. Many of them were involved in helping the new government when the Reagan administration launched its war against Nicaragua. When the Reagan administration was found guilty of violating international law in its war against Nicaragua by the International Court of Justice (ICJ) at The Hague and ordered to pay reparations, our allies encouraged Reagan to stop the war. But when Reagan kept right on waging a war that the International Court of Justice had deemed illegal, and which our allies knew amounted to nothing more than terrorism against a civilian population, our allies folded. They allowed US conservatives to destroy Nicaragua's revolution.

While the Reagan administration and conservatives were violating international law to promote their unnecessary war, many Democrats in Congress tried to stop them. The US Congress passed specific laws forbidding Reagan from continuing to wage his war against Nicaragua, but the Reagan administration simply ignored these laws. The war against Nicaragua proved that no one could stop a determined conservative administration from waging an unnecessary war anywhere it chose.

All of the tactics developed by the Corporate Feudalists in Nicaragua were later repeated in the first and second wars against Iraq. First, conservatives lied to get us into those wars. Then they manipulated the media into covering their lies as if they were facts. As in the war against Nicaragua, they rallied conservative Evangelical leaders in the United States to support these wars, and they ignored international opinion and lied to the United Nations. Finally, George W. Bush's administration used fear and anger to sway US public opinion and lied to Congress to manipulate a vote authorizing the invasion of Iraq right before US national elections.

Many people who believe the second Gulf War was unnecessary still think the first Gulf War, launched by the first President Bush, was justified. The facts tell a different story, however. Prior to the first Gulf War, Iran and Iraq had been engaged in a ten-year war. Iran had become a revolutionary fundamentalist Islamic state, and Iraq was a secular Muslim dictatorship. US policy basically was to let these two countries fight it out but to make sure Iran did not win in the end. The United States did aid Iraq, but not enough to help it win outright. Iraq, in fact, served US interests by acting as a buffer between Iran, as it attempted to export its revolution, and the rest of the region. Kuwait, Saudi Arabia, and many other US allies also helped Iraq to defeat Iran.

One way countries like Kuwait helped Saddam Hussein wage the war against Iran was by providing loans to his country. When the war was over, Iraq found itself with a larger debt than it could afford to pay. Saddam Hussein first tried to get the countries that had lent him money to wage his war against Iran to forgive the debts completely or at least renegotiate the terms. He also asked Kuwait to enter into discussions at the World Court about settling a long-running border dispute that affected a large oil field Iraq claimed but Kuwait was drilling.

Saddam Hussein knew he had provided a great service to Kuwait and the rest of the region in ending Iran's attempt to spread its revolution and expected the countries that had helped finance his war to be grateful. What he got instead were personal insults from the Emir of Kuwait and a declaration that Kuwait had no intention of seeking resolution of its border dispute and planned to continue taking oil from land Iraq claimed as its own.

Saddam Hussein then expressed his frustration to the United States, which he believed was his ally. This is where the lies started in earnest. Saddam Hussein openly informed the US ambassador to Iraq, April Glaspie, that he was considering taking action against Kuwait but first wanted to know the US position. The ambassador informed him that the United States had no opinion on Arab-Arab conflicts and that the issue was not associated with America.

Saddam Hussein then invaded Kuwait, and the next day President George H. W. Bush made his "line in the sand" speech, telling Saddam Hussein to get out of Kuwait or else. By making a public demand, Bush knew Saddam Hussein would not leave before the deadline expired because no dictator could afford to lose face in the eyes of his people.

Once Saddam Hussein's troops were safely stuck in Kuwait, the Bush administration needed to get congressional and US public support for a war. Many famous public relations firms were hired to influence the US Congress and engage in numerous false propaganda operations to win public support. One of the most lasting images was of a fifteen-year-old girl testifying before Congress about how she had seen Iraqi soldiers dumping babies out of incubators at a Kuwait hospital. Then there was the supposed US intelligence claiming that Iraqi tanks were gathering on the border of Saudi Arabia in preparation for an attack against that country.

The propaganda was enough to get US Congressional and public support, as well as the support of many allied nations throughout the world. Only after the war had been safely started did some of the truth come out, and then only for those who were looking. Ambassador Glaspie, who before the war had denied telling Saddam Hussein that the United States would not get involved, was called up to Congress after transcripts surfaced in which it appeared that she had, in fact, give him the green light. The woman who famously told Congress and the nation about the incubators was actually the Kuwait ambassador's daughter, who had been given the story and coached on how to tell the tale by one of the public relations firms. This story had been made up, as well as the intelligence about Iraqi tanks gathering on the border, to mislead Congress, the US public, and the rest of the world so they would support a completely unnecessary war.

Then came the second Gulf War, started by President George W. Bush, which followed the same pattern with the same results. The Bush administration claimed that Iraq was involved in the 9/11 attacks, that it had proof Iraq had weapons of mass destruction, and that it even knew where these supposed weapons were. Further, the Bush administration claimed that Al Qaeda had been operating in Iraq prior to the US invasion. To demonstrate that these lies were intelligence failures, the Bush administration created a separate intelligence department within the Pentagon, headed by a right-wing zealot who had openly called for going to war against Iraq long before 9/11. All of these lies that led us into the second war with Iraq have now been exposed, but the criminals who told them continue to claim they were just following bad intelligence.

The predictable result of these unnecessary wars launched by conservative administrations included another massive transfer of wealth from ordinary middle-class taxpayers to a few Corporate Feudalists and the ongoing drain of the US Treasury. Combined with the other parts of the plan for Corporate Feudalism, the second war in Iraq just about finished the job started by Reagan thirty years before. Today, the

US Treasury is empty, the US debt is massive, the US middle class is on life support, and the United States is beginning to look like a feudal republic.

The Corporate Feudalists have a proven track record when it comes to selling and starting unnecessary wars. Do you think you found a better way to sell unnecessary wars to the public than the plan outlined above? Or do you think the plan they used was perfect for the job?

CHAPTER 16

Step Eleven: Conning the Evangelical Church

What would you do? Your task for this step is to find a large group of people who will support your goals without knowing what those goals really are. If you agree with the Corporate Feudalists that the Evangelical Church is your best bet, how would you convince its members to join your cause?

Every revolution needs a core of committed individuals to foster and support its cause. The conservative revolution designed to eliminate the US middle class was no exception.

But it would have been impossible to find a very large group of people committed to destroying the middle class. Once again the originators of the plan for Corporate Feudalism needed to get creative, which they did.

Politics is all about making coalitions, and the coalition the conservatives created to eliminate the middle class was impressive. They started with a small group of people who would actually benefit from eliminating the middle class. Although this group was minuscule in number, it possessed the unlimited wealth necessary to carry out their plan for the Reagan Revolution and Corporate Feudalism. An additional part of this coalition consisted of Republicans who would support any Republican at any time no matter what. In addition, there were members of the right wing who just liked the idea of attacking and destroying government as a matter of principle, not realizing the consequences to the middle class. But all of these groups together amounted to nowhere near the numbers needed to cause a conservative revolution.

Fortunately for the conservatives, they discovered the Evangelical Church. For many years prior to the Reagan Revolution, Evangelical churches throughout the United States had been growing in number. These churches were fiercely independent, but as a group they had found a formula for drawing new people into their fold. They made church fun, exciting, and relevant.

The term "Evangelical" refers to spreading the teachings of Christ as presented in the Gospels, which is what members of these churches were doing. Many of the fastest-growing Evangelical churches at that time were the first to incorporate modern technology into Sunday morning services. Instead of the old-style church services, there were slide shows, entertaining visuals, and modern music, often including Christian-style rock music for teenagers, complete with electric guitars and drum sets. In addition, at many of the largest Evangelical churches the gospel of prosperity could be heard, reassuring middle-class Americans about financial security. This gospel teaches that if you are faithful and give to God, God will return the favor ten or even one hundred times over. To demonstrate this gospel of prosperity, the leaders of the largest congregations could be seen driving Rolls-Royces, flying their own planes, and sporting gold rings on their fingers. To parishioners, the message was clear: anyone could be rich as long as they were faithful to God, which included giving generously to the church. So the Evangelicals' numbers grew and grew, coming primarily from the white middle class.

Prior to the Reagan Revolution most people had not heard of the Evangelical movement. This is partly because while Evangelicals were committed to spreading God's Word in a way that increased their church memberships, they were also committed to staying away from politics. Evangelicals believed, with good reason, that politics was a dirty business and the best way to avoid being contaminated by it was to steer clear of it.

But the Evangelicals were discovered by politicians and the media anyway during the election of Jimmy Carter, who himself was an Evangelical. Carter attended church regularly. He taught Sunday school, tithed, and he was extremely successful—the sort of person any Evangelical church would have been proud to have as a member. During Carter's campaign for president, the media picked up on his Evangelical roots. Suddenly, stories started appearing about who Evangelicals were, what they believed, and whether they would help Carter get elected. For the national media, discovering Evangelicals was like discovering Martians on Earth—something new and unexpected in their midst. This media attention publicly elevated the status of Evangelicals. While Carter and the Democrats did not court them, in the end Carter was elected with their help, since the Evangelicals considered him one of their own.

During the Carter campaign, Evangelicals were also discovered by the people who created the plan for Corporate Feudalism. The conservatives and the Corporate Feudalists correctly perceived that Evangelicals could serve as the missing core of support for elimination of the middle class. Here was a large and growing body of people who were essentially morally and politically innocent—with no deep political alliances and committed, for the most part, to moral decency. Perhaps most importantly, for the conservatives, this community was motivated by faith.

The conservatives' plan to hook the Evangelicals was simple and straightforward. They identified a few issues of importance to Evangelicals and made these issues their own. Where these issues were involved, the conservatives even adopted the specific language of the Evangelicals. Never before had Evangelicals been courted so directly, and never before had a US political party devised a strategy and language to align itself with a religious group.

Evangelicals were not asked to change their beliefs, which they would not have done anyway. Instead, they were told that conservative Republicans held the very same beliefs. In many cases, this was not true, but when has the truth had anything to do with a good con?

And not only were conservatives, Republicans, and Evangelicals portrayed as all being in the same boat, but liberals and Democrats were demonized as godless enemies who were trying to destroy everything in which the Evangelicals and conservatives believed. However, even with such a clever strategy, the conservatives' plan to use Evangelicals as a core group of support to eliminate the middle class might not have worked without the help of televangelists.

As the Evangelical Church had grown and prospered, the importance of television preachers known as televangelists had increased as well. Because Evangelical churches were independent, they did not have strong hierarchical connections. According to Evangelical theology, God communicates with individual believers; the idea that a person like the pope or another member of the church hierarchy could speak for an individual congregation was unacceptable. Thus each congregation, even within strong denominations like Southern Baptists, was given wide latitude in determining its own policies. For example, Evangelical congregations selected their own pastors, as opposed to letting the church hierarchy appoint people to fill these positions. The advantage of this practice was that it assigned more power and control to individual congregations. The disadvantage was that it resulted in a leadership vacuum at the top. By the late 1970s and early 1980s, the televangelists were more than ready and willing to fill this vacuum.

For many years, Christian programming had been televised both locally and nationally, usually in the form of Sunday morning services. But these services were not designed for television; they were simply broadcast as a service to the local community. What the televangelists realized was that they could use the same technologies employed in Evangelical churches to create made-for-television church spectaculars every week. These church spectaculars would prove to be extremely lucrative. Suddenly, a few preachers were able to reach not hundreds or even thousands of believers on a single Sunday, but millions. The wealth and power created by and for these television preachers was phenomenal, and as a result, televangelists were immediately incorporated into the plan for Corporate Feudalism.

Now millionaires who had amassed great power and wealth, televangelists were preaching the gospel of prosperity, which was fully consistent with the plan for Corporate Feudalism. If these television preachers would simply amplify the issues selected by conservatives while ignoring the issues advocated by liberals, the conservative revolution's con would be complete. In exchange, these televangelists would be given access to President Reagan and all the perks and prestige that go along with being power insiders. This, in turn, would further elevate the televangelists' status with their audiences.

Before conservative Republicans had convinced Evangelicals that they were all one big happy family, Evangelicals had been interested in a great many moral issues. Because they read their Bibles and attended Bible studies, they often encountered passages about helping the poor and sharing what they had with the less fortunate. But once under the influence of the conservatives' con, Evangelicals found themselves being led down a different path. Instead of helping the poor or fighting for the oppressed, as in earlier days, they ended up preaching about abortion, homosexuality, or what liberal Democrats were doing to destroy the moral fiber of the nation.

After thirty years of being led by a group of conservative politicians claiming to be on their side, Evangelicals have lost a great deal. In fact, not since the Louisiana Purchase of 1803 has one group given so much and received so little in return. Evangelicals have unknowingly become the core supporters of the Corporate Feudalists' plan to eliminate the US middle class. As they had rightly recognized before being manipulated to help with the agenda of Corporate Feudalism, politics is indeed a dirty business. And in the end, the faith of the Evangelicals blinded them. Placing one's faith in God can be rewarding and fulfilling. Placing one's faith in people who claim to be on your side or God's side, is a different matter altogether.

When it was learned that several of the conservative politicians leading the impeachment against then-President Bill Clinton were, hypocritically, involved in their own marital infidelities and other unethical behaviors, Evangelicals remained faithful to the conservative politicians. When one conservative politician after another was found to be leading a life completely at odds with what he or she publicly professed, Evangelicals remained faithful to the conservatives. When open theft and lying at the highest levels of the conservative movement were exposed, the Evangelicals remained faithful to the conservatives. When it became obvious that George W. Bush had lied to the American public to justify the war in Iraq, the Evangelicals remained faithful to him. Even when several televangelists themselves were exposed as liars, perverts, or rapists, the Evangelical community continued to support conservative politicians.

Today, Evangelicals find themselves in a difficult position. Many of the promises they received from the conservatives have not been kept, and the information on which they were based has been proven false. Conservative politicians they were conned into supporting have been found to be no more moral than their liberal counterparts and often much less so. Policies conservatives advocated that were supposed to help the middle class have instead destroyed it. Now, with many Evangelicals fighting financially to survive, some are beginning to wonder what really happened. The old prosperity gospel no longer seems as true as it once did.

Thirty years is a long time to believe in something that turns out to be false, particularly when politicians used the power of faith to mislead the believers. While Evangelicals' faith in God may not be shaken, their faith in the conservative politicians who claimed they were doing God's work may ultimately crumble. But for the purpose of eliminating the middle class and bringing about Corporate Feudalism, the damage has already been done.

Did you think of a large group of people other than Evangelicals available thirty years ago to use as the core of support for the plan to eliminate the middle class? If you agreed that Evangelicals were the best group to accomplish this task, could you think of a better way to turn them into unquestioning supporters than the strategies discussed in this chapter? Or do you think the strategies employed were the best means for accomplishing this goal?

CHAPTER 17

Step Twelve: Developing a Policy of Lying

W hat would you do? Your goal for this step is to create a strategy that allows your spokespeople to keep telling a lie even after it has been exposed as false—that is, to develop a policy of lying.

It is no secret that governments lie, some more than others. Dictatorships can lie as much as they want. They control the military and the media. Who is going to stop a dictatorship from lying?

It is harder to lie in a democracy with a free media, at least in theory. In a democracy, if you are caught in a big enough lie you can be thrown out of office. So the lies told in a democracy tend to be smaller and more difficult to expose than in a dictatorship. For example, you can lie about enemy casualties in a war without getting into trouble. You can lie about other peoples' motives for their actions. In a democracy, however, to openly lie about things that can be proven false is very risky. At least it used to be.

In some ways, the conservatives' development of a policy of lying was the boldest part of the plan for Corporate Feudalism. Like other parts of the plan, destroying the US middle class would have been impossible without it. The Corporate Feudalists discovered that a lie is a lie only if someone calls it one. Beginning with the Reagan administration, they simply took control of the debate so they could lie whenever it suited their purposes.

First, the Corporate Feudalists had to gain control of the media, as discussed earlier. Then they had to make sure everyone on their team repeated the same lies, regardless of how foolish they sounded in the face of contradictory facts or how often they were confronted with the truth. And they had to call anyone who disagreed with their lies a liar. What the Corporate Feudalists counted on was moderation from their enemies, and that is just what they received. If the major media had insisted that the Reagan administration's claims were provably false or if the Democrats in Congress had been bold enough to call a lie a lie, the entire plan would have failed.

Unfortunately, neither the media nor the Democrats realized that Reagan was simply the movie star mouthpiece for the Corporate Feudalists' plan to eliminate the middle class. Early on in the Reagan administration, the media pointed out

inconsistencies or seeming impossibilities in Reagan's statements. But his administration carried out its plan regardless,
after which his lies were overlooked, downplayed, or excused
as mere exaggeration. There were a number of reasons for this.
As mentioned earlier, Reagan was charming and believable,
which is why he had been selected by the Corporate Feudalists
as cheerleader-in-chief. While he was often considered a bit
goofy, he still came across as grandfatherly and harmless. Like
the media, the Democrats, too, were caught up in the Reagan
charm, even if they thought he was a bit daft. Who could take
seriously a president who openly claimed that trees caused
more pollution than automobiles?[1]

Further, as ownership and regulatory rule changes allowed
the media to become more centralized and less independent,
they became less willing to effectively expose the continuing
lies. Moreover, the relative civility in American politics during
the 1980s and beyond didn't allow a decent politician to
openly call another politician a liar. Consequently, the pattern
of accepting obvious lies as fact became the norm for the thirty
years leading up to the present. There is no more obvious
example of this pattern of accepting lies as fact than Democrats'
acceptance of the Bush administration's lies during the lead-up
to the wars in Iraq. The lies leading to the second Iraq war were
provable and obvious, and the consequences enormously
costly. But even then most Democrats and the media were
unable to call a lie a lie. On the other hand, for thirty years
congressional Republicans led, often unknowingly, by
Corporate Feudalists have shown no reluctance to call the
Democrats liars if the Democrats pointed out inconsistencies
or obvious falsehoods in Republican dogma.

It seems Democrats just have not been able to tell the
difference between civility and criminality and have had

difficulty comprehending the broader intent of conservatives' lies. In fact, because it took so long for many congressional Democrats to understand why anyone would want to destroy the middle class they have remained unable to see it even as it is being done.

What made this step of the plan for Corporate Feudalism work was its boldness. Rather than starting off telling one lie and sticking to it, Reagan espoused several lies, and he was able to count on the congressional Republicans to support him. In fact, many Republican policies of today are based on fabricated so-called facts that were first created during the Reagan administration.

For example, the conservatives' lies about Nicaragua were bold because they were obvious. Nicaragua's elections were monitored by the entire world and certified as fair; Reagan called them a sham. Reagan portrayed Nicaragua as a totalitarian dungeon with its people living in fear of their government; the Nicaraguan government was arming all of its citizens with machine guns to defend themselves. Reagan claimed that Nicaragua had imported Soviet-made MiG aircraft into the country, but these so-called MiGs turned out to be farm equipment. At the time, every reporter on the ground could see that Reagan was lying and many wrote stories about it, but the reporters were attacked for their efforts and soon gave up on this type of reporting.

While the lies about Nicaragua were easy to prove, the bigger lies aimed at eliminating the middle class were more subtle though just as bold, such as the lies about cutting taxes for the rich, increasing military spending, and supposedly balancing the budget all at the same time. Reagan and the Republicans called this phenomenon trickle-down and supply-side economics. George H. W. Bush famously labeled supply-side economics "voodoo economics" before Reagan was elected, when a host of respected economists had demonstrated that trickle-down economics would never work.

However, to counter these claims the Corporate Feudalists had their right-wing economists explain how trickle-down economics was going to work and why. By the time record budget deficits appeared, most reporters and citizens alike had forgotten the false promises leading up to the deficits, or were simply unable or unwilling to see the obvious connection. By claiming that cutting taxes for the rich would help the economy and then running up huge budget deficits to pay for the tax cuts, it appeared to many who weren't paying close attention that the system was working. However, in retrospect we can prove that the tax cuts associated with trickle-down economics led directly to the massive budget deficits and the financial meltdown of 2008. We can also prove that every economic success claimed by the Republicans was paid for by the US Treasury-gutting plan of creating massive budget deficits. In addition, we can demonstrate that every time the Republicans initiated another round of tax cuts for the rich the deficits increased and the Republicans claimed victory.

Equally bold was the lying used to garner support for global free market initiatives launched during the Reagan Revolution. Reagan and the Republicans insisted that eliminating US tariffs and other protections for US workers would help the economy. They put forth a theory stating that unregulated capitalism would work in international markets by opening up new customer bases for American manufacturing, knowing full well that global labor competition would destroy America's manufacturing base. Again, they had the power and prestige of a popular president to support their theory, and they had their economists who could explain how and why it would be beneficial to the middle class. However, on the other side of the debate were many respected economists saying that Reagan and the Republicans' economic policies couldn't possibly work. How could US middle-class workers compete with overseas workers willing to earn three dollars a day? It just didn't make sense.

As the trade imbalance between the United States and other countries became unsupportably high and led to record-setting budget deficits, Republicans continued to insist that global free trade was succeeding. Many people still believe that global free trade and the Republican energy policy instituted under Reagan have been good for the US middle class because the Corporate Feudalists have repeated the same story for thirty years. Thirty years ago the assumption was that if the radical economic system proposed by Reagan failed we would simply return to the nation's system of tariffs and import controls that had worked for many decades. But up to this point Corporate Feudalists have successfully avoided any attempts to return to more sane trade policies by insisting that their plan is working.

A policy of lying and deception also was used to discredit beneficial environmental and energy policies. When Reagan and the Republicans took control of Washington, they consistently repeated lies about environmental protection and energy that would take many years, and in some cases decades, to disprove. The basic approach to the environment started by Reagan and continued by Republicans to this day is that there is no real problem—with the possible exception of environmentalists.

By the time Reagan was elected to office, America had faced its first energy crisis. People with any foresight had glimpsed the future and realized that oil was a finite resource. Prior to Reagan, President Carter had begun to lead the nation away from fossil fuel dependency. He had called for the United States to start conserving energy and to become a leader in pursuing and generating clean energy through technologies like wind and solar. In addition, Carter had instituted tax breaks and other economic incentives for US companies to begin large-scale manufacturing of these alternative technologies. He had even installed solar collectors on the White House roof to demonstrate how easy and possible it was for everyone to begin weaning themselves away from oil and move toward cleaner, more plentiful energy alternatives.

However, Reagan and the Republicans eliminated every energy program Carter had initiated. They claimed that all the talk about an energy crisis was just doom and gloom. Reagan asserted that there was no energy shortage but rather plenty of oil, coal, and nuclear power and, if we just kept doing what we had been doing all along, everything would be great. Reagan eliminated the tax breaks for alternative energy development. He also ripped the solar panels off the White House roof, claiming they were unsightly. He discouraged any talk about conservation and instead supported conspicuous consumption. In the process, he led the nation back to the days of complete dependence on traditional energy sources. Today, Republicans continue to fight every attempt to encourage energy conservation or nontraditional energy sources, including wind and solar technologies.

Even if it could be argued that Republicans believed oil was limitless, energy conservation was unnecessary, alternative energy was silly, or giving tax breaks to oil companies to perpetuate the old system was the best energy policy, there is no doubt that the Republican energy policy has had the same effect as other Reagan administration policies based on lies. By focusing on providing tax breaks to big oil companies and encouraging US dependence on oil-based technologies, the transfer of wealth from the middle class to the very wealthy has continued unabated.

The growing industries established in the past thirty years to produce wind generators and solar panels have been developed in Europe and China, not the United States as Carter had planned. Clean energy manufacturing jobs that could and should have been created in the United States were simply transferred overseas when Republicans eliminated the tax breaks established to help those industries get started. While eliminating these tax breaks was bad for the US economy, it was good if you were working to dissolve the middle class. The last thing you need if your goal is to get rid of the US manufacturing sector is a brand-new category of manufacturing jobs.

Thirty years of Republican energy policy has seriously wounded the US auto industry as well. In its fight against improved fuel efficiency standards, it encouraged US automakers to continue focusing on gas-guzzling vehicles. Consequently, while our foreign competitors have produced more and more energy-efficient vehicles, US automakers still manufacture vehicles that depend on unlimited and inexpensive oil supplies.

When Republicans gained the White House and both houses of Congress in 2002, they created new tax breaks specifically designed to encourage the production and sale of large gas-guzzling vehicles, including Hummers. This further encouraged US automakers to stay the course with their inefficient monster trucks and SUVs. Thus it was no surprise that US automakers were thrown into chaos and near failure when the inevitable oil price increases surfaced. It was also no surprise that the Republicans who had encouraged the auto companies to build big gas hogs were the same ones calling for the auto companies to file for bankruptcy and eliminate their union-backed middle-class workforce.

Successive Republican politicians have called environmentalists alarmists, socialists, communists, and even terrorists. The basic Republican policy toward the environment has been to lie and deny. An environmentalist once challenged Reagan to a duel where he would stay in a closed garage with a tree while Reagan stayed in a closed garage with a running car to see who would ask to be let out first. Reagan, of course, declined the offer. But the Republican environmental plan was all about perception management. The facts didn't really matter. For thirty years, conservatives have been able to ignore scientific evidence of global climate change by finding scientists who would support their agenda by claiming it is all a big hoax. This task is easy to accomplish by looking for scientists who are on the payroll of a polluting industry. Whenever science is involved, doubt is possible, and the Republicans took the doubt about environmental science to new heights.

But recent censorship of scientists by the George W. Bush administration suggests that Republicans know their environmental policies are based on lies. One of the major environmental efforts put forth by the George W. Bush administration was silencing all government scientists. In the process, right-wing politicos with no scientific background were given authority to censor and edit scientific papers written by government scientists. Other well-known and respected scientists on the government payroll had their work suppressed and were ordered by right-wing political appointees not to speak with the media.

Unfortunately, scientific censorship was not limited to government scientists. Much of the nongovernmental scientific research conducted in the United States was affected as well, especially federally funded private and university research. The same political litmus test used to silence government science was used in selecting which projects to fund and which to cut. If the conservatives believed what they were saying, why did they go to so much trouble to have right-wing political appointees with no scientific background censor the scientists?

What does lying about environmental protection have to do with the plan for Corporate Feudalism? First, undermining policies focused on environmental protection has the effect of transferring more wealth to the Corporate Feudalists because the less they spend on environmental safeguards, the more profit they pocket. Second, a healthy environment is a middle-class concept. In a corporate feudal republic, those at the top would simply live where it's clean. They would have no concern about places where the general public lives. If members of the general public got sick and died, there would always be plenty more to replace them. Overall, there is no doubt that Republican energy policy has led the nation toward Corporate Feudalism and the elimination of the middle class.

The lies begun during the Reagan administration and continued to this day have had an enormous impact on the American electorate. Many people are finally waking up to the reality that they have been lied to for years, although they still don't know why. A large segment of the US population knows, for example, that the Bush administration intentionally deceived them to wage war in Iraq. While the Republicans have tried to blame it on faulty intelligence, millions of Americans know the truth, and many are beginning to spot the new lies as they are introduced. Even so, the damage wreaked by thirty years of unchallenged lies is tremendous.

To recognize how this policy of lying has worked over time, we need only listen to any political discourse. We might hear that President Obama is a socialist. "Oh really, by what definition?" a news anchor could have asked but didn't. Or that the president was born in Kenya. Did anyone in the media call this an outright lie? How about the fact that the economic-stimulus bill of 2009 neither created nor saved any jobs? In today's world outright provable lies flow freely and no one is held accountable for even the worst of them.

Did you think of better strategies for getting away with openly lying about the effects of economic and energy policies than the one developed by the Corporate Feudalists? Or do you agree that the strategies they employed were the best means for accomplishing their goals?

CHAPTER 18

Step Thirteen: Exploiting Lack of Accountability

What would you do? Your goal for this step is to make sure Corporate Feudalists are not held accountable when the middle class crumbles. Can you create a better strategy to shift the blame and responsibility than the one used by the Corporate Feudalists?

The Corporate Feudalists figured out how to use the inherent lack of accountability at the top of our political system to promote their anti–middle-class agenda. They realized that politicians and others could get away with lying and breaking the law as long as they weren't caught doing anything too partisan.

Without this lack of accountability, the plan for Corporate Feudalism would never have gotten off the ground. If either the Democrats or the media had held the Reagan administration accountable for the initial lies the administration proffered, we would not have had to live through thirty years of conservative lies about trickle-down economics, unregulated capitalism, and global free trade. But faced with a popular president and congressional Republicans who were willing to keep repeating the same lies even when they had been proven false, both the Democrats and the media folded. They were afraid to say, "You're lying." The entire US middle class is now paying the price for their fear.

We cannot blame the Corporate Feudalists for creating the lack of accountability at the top in our political system; it has always been there to some degree. Since the United States began as a federal constitutional republic through rebellion against the rule of Great Britain, perhaps we can blame British royalty for our leaders' lack of accountability. Further, the presidential pardon, which legally empowers the president to grant reprieve to lawbreakers and wrongdoers as he sees fit, may also play a role.

In addition, the fact that the maximum legal punishment for a US president is removal from office, or impeachment, which is an extremely difficult, disruptive, and costly process for the nation, likely plays a role. Essentially, the president can engage in any activity unless it is so obviously illegal and partisan that the other side is compelled to act, as was the case in the Watergate scandal of the 1970s, the effects of which led to the resignation of President Richard Nixon.

The threat of impeachment can also be used when the party out of power wages an all-out partisan witch-hunt, like the Republicans did against Bill Clinton for sexual indiscretion. For ordinary nonpartisan crimes, however, impeachment is usually not worth the trouble. Yet even impeachment does not amount to accountability. Think how happy criminals would be if they knew that their punishment for breaking the law was to be fired with a pension—not exactly a harsh sentence.

Looking at lack of accountability during the Reagan administration helps reveal how this factor was used to advantage by the Corporate Feudalists. During the Reagan administration, the Corporate Feudalists understood that only two groups had the power to hold the president accountable—the Democrats and the media. During the Nixon administration, the Democrats had proved they could be roused to action if a blatant partisan attack against them were discovered. But the Corporate Feudalists rightly realized that, short of a partisan attack that would harm them directly, the Democrats could be cowed into submission. The Democrats of thirty years ago saw themselves as legislators, not fighters. They would fight the good fight during the day and socialize with their Republican colleagues at night, thinking that Congress was one big happy family. The Democrats were also used to incremental changes. For many years, they had controlled Congress simply because the middle class correctly perceived them as their allies and Republicans as allies of big business and big money. When the Corporate Feudalists used Reagan to capture a large chunk of the middle-class vote, the Democrats didn't know what hit them. In lieu of the incremental changes they were used to, the Democrats faced a well-planned and well-funded revolution, leaving them overwhelmed.

As a popular Republican president who had garnered considerable middle-class support, Reagan and his administration promoted all kinds of radical plans and programs that would have seemed impossible just two years before. But when Democrats resorted to their basic position of trying to compromise they were steamrolled. Had the Corporate Feudalists attempted to implement their radical economic plans one at a time, they would have been stopped. The Republicans, by issuing a tsunami of changes based on the hopes and dreams of the middle class, in combination with a well-orchestrated campaign of half truths and lies, swept away the Democrats' objections in the flood.

The other group with the power to hold the president accountable during the Reagan administration was the media. However, several factors worked against the media's intervening too directly in exposing the Reagan myth, as discussed in chapters 6 and 7. Of particular relevance was the fact that corporate media owners were benefiting directly from deregulation proposals advanced by Reagan.

If the media printed a story contradicting the president, the president would accuse the media of being biased. They were either unwilling or simply unprepared to go toe-to-toe with an administration that was intent on using all the tools in its possession to fight back. So the media began to print what both sides said, without trying to verify the actual truth. Because Reagan was such a popular and telegenic president, and because the Corporate Feudalists had begun taking over the supposedly free media, the Republicans' side of a story was repeated much more often than the Democrats' side. And as all good propagandists know, the key to success is repetition.

To see even more concretely how lack of accountability has led directly to eliminating the middle class and brought us to the brink of Corporate Feudalism, let us review some of the lies explored in earlier chapters. The case of Nicaragua is illustrative. Congressional Democrats were adamantly opposed to Reagan's war in Nicaragua, using every legal channel available to stop the war. In response, the Reagan administration lied about what it was doing, ignored Congress, and violated US law in order to continue its attempts to overthrow the Nicaraguan government. It even went so far as to sell sophisticated weapons to our stated enemy Iran to fund the war in Nicaragua, which Congress had declared illegal and refused to finance.

When the scope of the Reagan administration's illegal activity was exposed, the Democrats tried to hold the administration's members accountable. However, they failed miserably. The Republicans in Congress stood behind the administration, ignoring the fact that laws had been broken. Wanting to appear statesmanlike, the Democrats picked moderates to lead their challenge, in contrast to the Republicans, who selected many of the most right-wing ideological members of their party to defend them. On one side, there was a very measured attempt to ascertain the facts; on the other, an impassioned ideological defense. Once again the Democrats ended up looking weak while the Republicans appeared strong.

Early on, the media provided accurate reporting, but when they were attacked directly and Reagan claimed that his actions were in the interest of national security, the media backed off. In the end, a few convictions were obtained, but then Reagan pardoned those who had been convicted, resulting in no accountability. Once again the government's lack of accountability went unpunished, and the Corporate Feudalists moved one step closer to implementing their plan for Corporate Feudalism.

By the time the Reagan administration's policies were found in violation of international law by the International Court of Justice (ICJ), the media were completely under the Republican administration's control. Never before had the United States been found in violation of international law or ordered to cease its activities and pay reparations for the damage it had done illegally. But neither the Democrats nor the media were able to use this incredible breach of trust with the American people to hold the Reaganites accountable. It was too late.

Much the same can be said about Reagan's economic theory known as trickle-down, or supply-side, economics. Trickle-down economics promised big tax cuts for the rich and a balanced budget for everyone else. However, implementation of this theory resulted in the beginning of massive budget deficits that have been crippling the United States to this day. No one responsible for this policy was held accountable. Once supply-side economics was shown to be failing, the public should have been informed. Long before now, every American should have known that the policy of cutting taxes for the wealthy caused massive budget deficits. Instead, for thirty years Republicans have continued to claim that trickle-down economics is working, which is true if your goal is to eliminate the middle class.

Lack of accountability also figured prominently in the Republicans' practices of deregulation and global free trade. The promise here was that the markets would regulate themselves and that global free trade would create millions of new jobs in the United States. When these promises failed to materialize, no one was held accountable except US taxpayers. When the unregulated savings and loan industries failed, US taxpayers were forced to bail them out in what was then the largest taxpayer bailout in history. Nor was Reagan's promise of the wonders of deregulation discredited. When America started losing its manufacturing base as a result of unregulated global free trade and the removal of protectionist tariffs, the media refused to expose the failings of these plans. Instead, we were treated to decades of "balanced" reporting.

The conservatives' stance toward US energy policy was the same as that toward trickle-down economics, deregulation, and global free trade. Reagan claimed that we did not need to conserve the country's energy resources or move away from our dependence on fossil fuels. For thirty years, Republicans have fought every effort to increase fuel economy standards for American cars. They have also successfully fought efforts to increase funding for clean, renewable energy sources like wind power and solar energy. But as the US auto industry nearly collapsed in the face of its more energy-efficient competition, the media failed to highlight the Republicans' thirty-year refusal to embrace energy efficiency or clean, alternative energy. Another important part of the conservatives' environmental policy has been to keep green technologies from taking hold. While the potential for creating an entirely new means for manufacturing involving green-related jobs has existed for three decades, much of this work is not easily exportable to foreign countries. If your goal is to destroy the US middle class, the last thing you want is entirely new locally based industries.

Conservative Republicans have waged an effective war against environmental protection ever since Reagan put anti-environmentalists in charge of the Environmental Protection Agency (EPA) and the Department of the Interior (DOI), where they suppressed legitimate science and produced reams of factually inaccurate and misleading pseudoscience without being held account-able for the disastrous results. Instead, their claims that global climate change is a hoax, or at least a controversial scientific theory, are given much more attention than they deserve based on the overwhelming scientific evidence to the contrary.

While the conservatives' environmental policies have not led directly to the elimination of the middle class, they have contributed to its decline. For one thing, these policies have helped discredit the United States throughout the rest of the world, making other countries much less sympathetic toward the United States as it begins to fail economically. As we will see in chapter 20, this is an instrumental step toward destroying the US middle class.

These are just a few examples of how the Corporate Feudalists have exploited the almost complete lack of government accountability that has existed since the Reagan Revolution. Now let us look at what should have happened and how a simple act of accountability could have stopped the entire plan for Corporate Feudalism in its tracks.

When the first conservative lies about Nicaragua surfaced, the media and the Democrats pointed out that statements by Reagan and the Republicans were false. But when the Reagan administration kept telling the same lies the media and the Democrats backed off. Had the media or the Democrats instead been willing to repeat the truth, eventually they would have had to label Reagan's fabrications as intentional falsehoods. Once this happened, the Reagan administration would have had to either stop lying or be called liars.

Once the media or the Democrats established that the Reagan administration was intentionally and repeatedly lying about Nicaragua, their other claims would have been examined for intentional falsehood as well. Then instead of having to wait thirty years to figure out that cutting taxes for millionaires increases the federal budget deficit, we could have learned it much sooner. Instead of having to wait until the US manufacturing base was severely crippled to learn that global free trade and the elimination of tariffs would undermine the middle class, we could have considered the possibility that conservatives were intentionally lying about the economy just as they were lying about Nicaragua. Instead of waiting until global climate change became impossible to deny before starting to work on solutions, we could have been moving forward to address the problems. Most importantly, if the conservatives had been held accountable when caught lying about a small war we could have avoided at least the second, if not both, of the US wars against Iraq. Likewise, if President H. W. Bush had known that he would be held accountable for telling lies to con the United States into the first war in Iraq, we would not have entered into that war or the second one.

If the thirty years since Reagan's rule have taught conservatives anything, it is that they will never be held accountable for their public actions. Political leaders can still get into trouble for stealing or for personal corruption issues, but just as they got away with lying to instigate unnecessary wars, so will they get away with promoting policies that will destroy the US middle class.

There is almost no accountability in American politics today. Do you think this is just par for the course or do you believe it is an integral component of the Corporate Feudalists' plan? If you believe the lack of accountability was part of the plan, can you think of a better way to avoid accountability than the one described above? Or do you think the Corporate Feudalists used the best strategy possible?

CHAPTER 19

Step Fourteen: Corrupting the Courts

What would you do? Your goal for this step is to secretly turn the US federal court system, including the US Supreme Court, into an ideologically conservative body. Perhaps someday you might need the Supreme Court to carry out a coup for you, or you might need legal cover to stay out of jail. You might even need the Supreme Court to say that corporations have the same rights as people but without the same responsibilities. Or you might need it to decide corporations have every right to buy as many politicians and elections as they can afford.

Corrupting the US court system was another integral part of the plan for Corporate Feudalism. Corporate Feudalists must have known that eventually members of the US middle class would realize they had been conned. A right-wing US court system could keep any legal action from stopping the process of eliminating the US middle class even when laws were being broken. In many ways, the strategy for corrupting the US court system was the same as the strategy for corrupting the media. Reagan and his team started by labeling the courts "too liberal." Then they set out to correct this supposedly liberal bias. They never said they were planning to turn the US court system into an ideologically right-wing body; according to the conservatives, they were simply working to correct the bias in the judicial system. But, as with other parts of the plan for Corporate Feudalism, the result was a radical departure from past practices, and from the outcomes they promised.

Beginning with the Reagan administration, the procedure for filling federal court appointments was significantly altered. Before the Reagan administration, the two most important qualifications for appointing a federal judge were previous experience and judicial temperament. Most of the federal judges selected by both parties were chosen because they were well respected in their field. This was especially true for Supreme Court appointees. It took many years for these men (it was all men back then) to prove themselves worthy of a lifetime Supreme Court appointment. Even the lesser federal judges were usually selected based on their experience, intelligence, and moderation.

This all changed with the Reagan Revolution. Regardless of their claim to seek balance in the federal courts, what

Reaganites set out to do was create an ideologically driven federal judiciary. Instead of well-respected moderates, conservatives started filling the courts with right-wing ideologues. Like other parts of the plan for Corporate Feudalism, the effects of this change did not become apparent overnight. But gradually the Corporate Feudalists succeeded in placing many young, far-right ideologues into federal judicial positions.

Filling the courts with right-wing ideologues was important to Corporate Feudalists for two reasons. First, it served as an insurance policy. From the beginning, Corporate Feudalists realized that to carry out their plan it might be necessary to break US laws. If they could get away with illegal proceedings through a lack of accountability or timidity from their opposition, they would not need the courts. But if they could not get away with illegal activities they would need a right-wing judiciary to at least buy them time until their plan for Corporate Feudalism had been fully implemented.

The second reason for filling the courts with conservative ideologues was even more important and involved the Supreme Court coup of 2000—the Supreme Court decision that resulted in George W. Bush's election to office. It is hard to imagine that Corporate Feudalists planned the Supreme Court coup back when they were launching their plan thirty years ago, but we do know they were farseeing. Perhaps they realized they would need the Supreme Court to push their plans for the elimination of the middle class over the top. Or maybe they were just lucky.

Filling the Supreme Court with conservatives did push the country toward the desired corporate feudal republic. By the time of the 2000 election, Reagan and President George H. W. Bush had appointed a majority of the Supreme Court justices. This was partly because the strategy for judicial appointments had shifted to appointing younger people, making the impact of any one ideologically motivated justice much more lasting. If congressional Democrats had had a spine, they would never have allowed ideologues like John Roberts, Clarence Thomas, and Samuel Alito Jr. to become Supreme Court justices. The Democrats knew—or should have known—that these three nominees were right-wing judicial activists. The Democrats also should have known that these justices were lying when they claimed they would respect past judicial precedent. There was plenty of evidence demonstrating that these justices were far-right procorporate activists long before they were appointed to the Supreme Court. Unfortunately, the Democrats just gave the Corporate Feudalists what they wanted. Once again, congressional Republicans were playing by the rules of Corporate Feudalism while the Democrats were still behaving like members of the old collegial Congress, deferring to the president's wishes because it was, after all, his turn to appoint judges.

While Reagan and President George H. W. Bush were unable to push all their ideologues through the confirmation process, they were able to confirm the least qualified justice ever to sit on the Supreme Court—Justice Clarence Thomas. This was done by exploiting the Democrats' fear of appearing prejudiced. The Republicans realized that some Democrats would find it impossible to vote against confirming a black justice to the Supreme Court, regardless of the candidate's extreme right-wing ideology, lack of judicial experience, or young age. Perhaps the Democrats hoped Thomas would change once he received his lifetime appointment. Or perhaps they were afraid that a vote against Thomas would alienate their African-American constituencies. Maybe they failed to realize how influential one young Supreme Court justice could be. Or it could be they felt that President George H. W. Bush would appoint a right-wing ideologue anyway, so what was the difference? Whatever the reasons, one thing is clear: over the past thirty years, whenever the Republicans had Supreme Court appointments to make, ideology became an increasingly important part of their selection criteria. At the same time, they successfully opposed every Democratic appointment that was anything other than moderate.

The Republicans' successful fight to ideologically control the Supreme Court was the single most important factor underlying its coup of 2000. For the first time in the history of the Supreme Court, the right-wing Court majority made a ruling they specifically stated they did not want used as precedent for future rulings. Why? Because the Court knew the decision was wrong, and it did not want some future Court using this decision to appoint someone the conservatives did not anoint.

What is known about the 2000 decision are the following facts. Nationwide, Al Gore received five hundred thousand more votes than George W. Bush. In Florida the Republicans intentionally removed at least fifty-five thousand legally registered Democrats from the voter rolls prior to the election. Most importantly, Al Gore would have won in Florida if a statewide recount had been allowed; instead, the conservative majority on the Supreme Court stepped in, selected Bush in a five-to-four split decision to stop Florida's recount, and changed the course of history. This unprecedented event probably accelerated the plan for Corporate Feudalism by at least a decade because a Gore administration would not have fully implemented all fifteen steps.

As discussed earlier, the Corporate Feudalists' fifteen-step plan to eliminate the US middle class and move the nation toward a corporate feudal republic began with the Reagan presidency. Reagan pursued the plan for Corporate Feudalism and implemented what he could, but at the time many of the plan's proposals were too radical to be accepted by the American public. President George H. W. Bush simply followed this plan with minor modifications. Clinton, a conservative Democrat whom the Republicans successfully labeled as liberal, ignored some of the elements of the plan but pushed forward many others. In particular, Clinton retained several of the Reagan-Bush tax cuts, continued to deregulate much of the financial sector, and, perhaps most importantly for the Corporate Feudalists, worked with congressional Republicans to pass the North American Free Trade Agreement (NAFTA), which, long advocated by conservatives, proved to be a disaster for the US middle class. Even 1992 Independent presidential candidate Ross Perot, considered by most a fiscal conservative, warned that NAFTA would create a "giant sucking sound" as American jobs and prosperity left the country. Despite these disasters, Clinton was not part of the plan for Corporate Feudalism; rather, his economic policies created a budget surplus and started to reduce the national debt, reversing one of the main achievements of his predecessors.

Most likely, an Al Gore presidency would have resulted in many of the same outcomes as Clinton's. While the Gore team would have accepted some of the false assumptions set forth by the plan for Corporate Feudalism, they would not have accepted all of them, and thus not every step of the plan for Corporate Feudalism would have been implemented.

The presidency that implemented the remaining steps of the Corporate Feudalists' plan was that of George W. Bush, who was elected to office only because a right-wing Supreme Court majority appointed him. Once in power, Bush made the Corporate Feudalists proud. He finished deregulating the banking and mortgage industries. He continued attacks on unions and middle-class workers. He led the nation into a couple of costly and unnecessary wars. He created unheard of international animosity toward the United States, and he sent the nation into the largest budget deficit in the history of the world—a substantial accomplishment. As a result of George W. Bush's presidency, all practical impediments to the Corporate Feudalists' plan to destroy the US middle class have been eliminated. The assumptions of Corporate Feudalism have been sold and the steps of their plan implemented. All that remains for the Corporate Feudalists to do is bankrupt the United States and take over, an event that could happen sooner than we think.

In addition to assuring that George W. Bush become president, the right-wing majority of the Supreme Court found the means to address what had historically been a problem unique to feudalism. Feudal lords of the past were family centered, which worked as long as the families remained vital. Arranged marriages between the children of feudal lords helped perpetuate the system. But because children often did not have the abilities of the parents, even the strongest, best-connected families eventually diminished.

However, the new feudal lords-in-waiting discovered a solution to this problem, and the right-wing majority of what has become the US "Extreme Court" repaired feudalism's fundamental flaw. In a sweeping and unprecedented ruling, the Court majority found that corporations have the same rights as individuals but not the same responsibilities. Corporations have been given protected limited liability that shields both the corporations and their owners from the consequences of their actions. There is no law that forces corporations to tell the truth or that limits their lifespans. According to the conservative

Supreme Court majority, there is also no law governing how corporations use their money to influence US thought, or even US elections. As such, the US Supreme Court, operating as a right-wing, ideologically based institution, has created a more perfect form of feudalism, one in which the "families" of feudal lords do not eventually weaken and die out. Thus no longer is there a need to replace a dying feudal lord with an incompetent family member; instead, the corporations' owners can hire whomever they want. The profits can still go to the new-style feudal lords, but the rules have fundamentally changed: as long as corporations continue to possess the rights of individuals without the responsibilities, there is no stopping them from continuing to accumulate wealth and power forever.

Now that the right-wing justices of the Supreme Court have shown just how far they are willing to go to overturn established American law, efforts should be made to impeach these justices for openly lying during their confirmation hearings, when they claimed they would respect past judicial precedent. But if there is one thing the Corporate Feudalists have learned in the past thirty years, it is that they will not be held accountable for their actions.

The majority of Supreme Court justices have become conservative judicial activists while conservatives scream about judicial activism. Did you think of a better way to control an entire branch of government and make America's highest court unaccountable and a rubber stamp for Corporate Feudalism than the one that was used? Or do you agree that the plan put to use worked to perfection?

CHAPTER 20

Step Fifteen: Bankrupting the United States

Following implementation of the other steps to Corporate Feudalism, bankruptcy pretty much happens automatically. But what would you do? Your goal for this step is to come up with a way to bankrupt the United States and the fifty state governments as well. Bankruptcy—the inability of an individual, family, company, or government to pay its bills and remain fiscally viable—will finish the job of using the existing wealth of the country to transition from a middle-class democracy to a corporate feudal republic.

Here we will examine both personal bankruptcy and bankruptcy of the US federal and state governments. Personal bankruptcy, causing people to fall out of the middle class permanently, began almost as soon as Reagan was elected. In his initial efforts to cut social programs to bankroll billionaire tax cuts and increased military spending, Reagan dramatically reduced funding to institutions that had cared for mental health patients, forcing thousands of mentally challenged people onto the streets and leading to the first great wave of American homelessness. Families without the means to take care of these people and advocates of the mentally challenged and homeless complained. But these groups had no real power and were unable to either stop the policy or make it important enough to raise the public's consciousness about this issue. While the general public may have noticed an increase in homelessness, the homeless do not have much of a voice in this society and, therefore, are easily ignored. In retrospect, however, this wave of homelessness can be seen as the first wave of the ever-expanding concentric circles of poverty directly attributable to the Reagan administration and the plan for Corporate Feudalism.

As was the tendency during the Reagan administration, the homeless were blamed for their impoverished circumstances. They were called lazy, stupid, and even accused of being criminals, and the fact that they were ill and needed treatment was ignored. Many were easy for the majority of white middle-class citizens to blame, especially minorities, reinforcing the "us versus them" mentality the other steps encouraged.

Despite economic difficulties, many people worked harder and longer to maintain their middle-class lifestyle, even as the rules were being changed and the means to remain productive members of the middle class were being eliminated.

Both partners in relationships were often forced to join the workforce full-time to remain members of the middle class for a while longer. Soon, though, it became necessary for one or both partners to work multiple jobs just to stay afloat financially. The message coming from the media, however, was that everything was great, so people falling behind blamed themselves and one another.

As the owners of US companies moved their manufacturing overseas and the US government sold assets to keep the economy viable, average Americans at first did not notice that the middle class was shrinking dramatically or that wages for working people had diminished every year since the Reagan Revolution had begun. People were told it was their problem and dealt with it in whatever way they could. They no longer had unions to protect them or even to help them understand what was happening. Instead, they had corporate-owned media telling them that it was their fault. This shrinking of the middle class has continued unabated and mostly unnoticed since the days of Ronald Reagan's presidency.

Only now, as the wealth of the nation is spent and the manufacturing sector is almost gone, are the full effects of the plan for Corporate Feudalism being realized. Today it is clear that this shrinking of the middle class has continued since the days of Ronald Reagan's presidency, leading to the current race to the bottom for US middle-class wages. Millions of homeowners have lost or are losing their homes to foreclosure because of the unscrupulous and often illegal efforts of a deregulated mortgage and banking industry. Untold others are falling out of the middle class because they cannot afford to pay their medical bills while living in the only developed middle-class country in the world that fails to provide some form of government-run national health care. More and more families are finding they cannot make ends meet. For many, even a minor change, like a dramatic increase in gasoline prices, is enough to push them over the financial edge.

As more and more people began falling out of the US middle class, they started to look for someone to blame. Foreign workers who were willing to work for less than the US middle-class wage became a popular target, and there were others as well. But people have not blamed the conservative policies making up the plan for Corporate Feudalism. It was, however, these conservative policies that sent the US manufacturing sector overseas and that encouraged competition with Third World workers with whom the US middle class couldn't possibly compete. And it was these conservative policies that convinced a large segment of the US middle class to believe that if people at the top were given more it would somehow trickle down to benefit them. As the US middle class itself trickles down into obscurity, it's about time for its members to realize that they have been conned. Unless you are one of those people who can appreciate the beauty of the con itself, it is not a pretty sight.

While personal bankruptcy causes great hardship for many and gradually eliminates the middle class, it does not by itself move the United States from a middle-class democracy to a corporate feudal republic. This transition requires a far more dramatic development—bankruptcy of the US federal and state governments. Usually for a change that dramatic to occur, a war is required, and if the plan for Corporate Feudalism succeeds it will be the first time a middle-class democracy has been reduced to a corporate feudal republic without a fight, let alone a war. It will prove that the US middle class was nothing more than a necessary detour on the road to increasing the wealth and power of a few individuals.

Is it possible to bankrupt the United States? Thirty years ago, anyone who suggested such a thing would probably have been locked up in one of the mental institutions Reagan eventually closed. Thirty years ago, the United States was the undisputed economic leader of the world. We produced more, exported more, and consumed more than any other nation, and we had the military power to protect this privilege. We also had the sometimes grudging respect of the free world that believed we were committed to living on the side of truth, justice, and liberty. That was before the Reagan Revolution and the plan for Corporate Feudalism, however. As the United States totters on the brink of financial ruin, several new circumstances brought to us by the Corporate Feudalists and their conservative representatives will make our economic recovery much more difficult this time around.

One important factor in bringing the United States closer to bankruptcy and making economic recovery more difficult is the sheer size of the national debt. Since Reagan was elected, Republicans have run up the largest debt in the history of the world (as chart 1 on page 4 illustrates). At the same time, the conservative policies of global free trade and the elimination of tariffs protecting American workers have resulted in the elimination of much of the US manufacturing sector. In the past, it was the manufacturing sector that generated the wealth necessary to pay off the national debt. Without the ability to generate wealth through manufacturing, we are now stuck trying to pay off the debt by selling assets and raw materials. This is why for the past several years we have heard of one deal or another involving a country like Dubai purchasing our ports, or some other nation or foreign business buying up other parts of the United States. If and when the conservatives are removed from power, the government will try to do what it can to remedy the situation. The government can infuse more money into the system in an effort to prime the economic pump, which worked in the past when consumer spending led to more middle-class jobs in the United States, resulting in more products to sell to US consumers. Now, however, due to global free trade and outsourcing, America's consumer spending creates more jobs for the Chinese, Mexican, and other Third World economies where the majority of corporate manufacturing is currently done. A few jobs in sales have been created at Wal-Mart and other retailers, as well as a few jobs in importing, unloading, and transporting these foreign-made goods to their final destinations. But none of these jobs creates the wealth necessary to keep the US economic engine running. None of these jobs creates the wealth necessary to pay off our national debt. None of these jobs creates the wealth necessary to pay middle-class wages and benefits over time. So this type of stimulus will provide only temporary, if any, relief to the once-powerful middle class. Unfortunately, the same is true for temporary job creation programs necessary to help with the immediate crisis of large-scale unemployment. Such programs use borrowed money, and the jobs do not create real wealth. Although they might play a positive role in repairing America's crumbling infrastructure, which, in turn, might provide other assets for America to sell as it tries to pay off its massive foreign debt, they will not generate the wealth necessary to reboot America's middle class. And any government spending of borrowed money that does not generate wealth will eventually lead the United States further into debt and that much closer to bankruptcy.

Another important factor making it difficult to reverse the effects of near bankruptcy and a disappearing middle class are conditions resulting from deregulation and privatization of government services. It was deregulation that allowed banks and mortgage companies to perpetrate the sham mortgage products leading first to the great housing bubble and, later, to the great housing collapse of 2008. Now, even as the US economy plummets due to banking and mortgage deregulation, the US government has been conned into borrowing billions more dollars to give to the very banks and mortgage companies that caused the crisis in hopes of keeping the economy afloat. By creating loans that forced millions of Americans to lose their homes in foreclosure, the banks were rewarded with direct payments from the taxpayers. This is, in fact, a perfect example of the ultimate goal of the fifteen steps—to transfer wealth from the 99 percent to the Corporate Feudalists.

Further, as privatization is increased, those remaining middle-class jobs in the government will be replaced by temporary jobs without benefits, stability, or meaningful accountability. These privatized jobs often cost the taxpayers more money for fewer services, which is good for the contractors but bad for US workers and the US economy in general.

Another factor that is making it difficult to reverse the effects of near bankruptcy is the extreme expense of waging unnecessary wars with no satisfactory justification given. The wars in Afghanistan and Iraq could and should have been avoided, but instead both were pursued. Some of the enormous amount of US taxpayer money spent in this effort is at least being used to make weapons and ammunition in a few of the remaining factories still paying middle-class wages. However, much more is being transferred to private contractors who outsource everything to the cheapest bidder anywhere in the world. For US taxpayers, these wars are digging an ever-deeper financial hole that can no longer be filled by the limited wealth now created in the United States.

The US middle class is currently in an economic downward spiral, with our country owing more money than it can afford to repay. The middle-class jobs originally created by unions fighting for middle-class wages in the manufacturing sector are mostly gone, having been transferred to Third World countries in response to the global free market. The jobs that are left for former US middle-class workers pay less and offer fewer benefits than the jobs of an earlier generation.

The remaining vestiges of middle-class success are now available to fewer and fewer people. The number of Americans who formerly had some type of health insurance and now have none has increased by millions. The quality of public schools in poor and once middle-class areas is declining rapidly. The number of formerly middle-class people who cannot afford to send their children to college has also increased at a dramatic rate. The unions, former leaders in promoting middle-class lives for their members and everyone else, are now weakened by massive US job losses due to global free trade and international outsourcing. The simple necessities of food, clean water, shelter, health care, and education have been put out of reach of millions of Americans who formerly made up the middle class. To try and maintain the middle-class lifestyle that Americans consider their birthright, many have gone into unsupportable credit card and other consumer debt. Many others now have no choice but to file for personal bankruptcy. The lifestyle taken for granted by members of the middle class thirty years ago is now limited to a much smaller group of professionals, who are watching their lifestyles deteriorate as well.

What would happen if the United States actually went bankrupt? Other large countries have gone bankrupt, such as Russia. Russia never had a vibrant middle class like the United States, or its impressive wealth of thirty years ago.

But Russia did have a large working class, as well as many natural resources. When Russia's government went bankrupt, the nation's resources were privatized and turned over to what Russia now calls the new oligarchs—a very small group of extremely affluent individuals who either own or control nearly all of the country's wealth. While the workers have less than they had before the economic collapse, the oligarchs have much more. As long as they support the government, it legalizes the oligarchs' activities and makes sure these individuals remain unchallenged. This is a very nice system, as long as you happen to be part of the oligarchy.

If the United States goes bankrupt, will we be any different from Russia? All of the nonessential government functions would have to be eliminated. There would be no money for health care or public education. To pay off the massive debt owed to other countries, something would have to be sold, such as America's natural resources. Who has enough money to buy these resources other than the Corporate Feudalists, who have been benefiting from the destruction of the US middle class since the days of the Reagan Revolution?

If the United States goes bankrupt, what would become of America's workers and other members of its former middle class? Those who survived would be reduced to the same state as workers in other feudal republics—trying to subsist on the crumbs handed out by the new feudal lords. The feudal lords would decide who works and who doesn't, who eats and who doesn't. Much like the Russian government, our government would be completely beholden to our own oligarchs, the Corporate Feudalists. In this role, the US government would protect the Corporate Feudalists and legally empower them to do whatever they deemed necessary. The United States would return to the way the Corporate Feudalists always thought it was supposed to be before unions created that pesky middle class during the Industrial Revolution—a world of haves and have-nots, where the few decide and the many abide.

None of this will have happened by accident. The course was set by the very clever designs of a small group of people who never wanted to share their wealth and power in the first place. These Corporate Feudalists were aided by a group of conservative politicians willing to serve as the hired help in exchange for a glimpse of the top and a little extra power. Destruction of the US middle-class economy has been an incremental process that has taken place over the course of thirty years as the steps to Corporate Feudalism have been gradually implemented. The majority of US citizens would never have supported the elimination of the middle class had they seen it coming. The majority will not voluntarily support the wholesale elimination of the US middle-class democracy either.

However, as Naomi Klein explains in her brilliant book *The Shock Doctrine: The Rise of Disaster Capitalism*, a country in economic crisis is forced to adopt policies it would never voluntarily accept.[1] And if the United States goes bankrupt, all of the old rules and requirements would automatically be eliminated. Bankruptcy would provide the perfect opportunity for the Corporate Feudalists to step in and completely reconfigure the US political system to their liking. The ensuing economic chaos would result in an end to all of the progressive social programs that conservatives have tried to eliminate for the past thirty years—Social Security, Medicare, environmental protection, public education, and housing assistance. Such economic chaos would also naturally lead to a major political crisis.

Some will ask: If our current political system has brought us to this economic chaos, wouldn't a different system be better—perhaps a more authoritarian system led by someone who promises to bring order and calm to the crisis? This is how authoritarian rule has developed in other countries. Thirty years ago there was no doubt we were immune to such a crisis. Even ten years ago the thought of our nation going bankrupt was unimaginable. But today the United States is staring into the abyss of bankruptcy, so what will stop the phenomenon Naomi Klein calls "disaster capitalism" from taking root here? Could it be that we are just such nice, hardworking, outstanding people that the Corporate Feudalists will decide to share their wealth and power with us, even though they no longer need to? Don't count on it.

It is still unknown whether the strategy to bankrupt the United States and state governments will be successful. What is known is that thus far the fifteen steps of the plan for Corporate Feudalism have worked brilliantly, and that they lead logically and directly to state and national bankruptcy as well as to the elimination of the middle class. The federal and state governments are already making drastic cuts to middle-class programs because of massive budget shortfalls. Perhaps the perception of bankruptcy will be sufficient to eliminate the middle class entirely.

The near bankruptcy the nation and several states have faced since 2008 has already gone a long way toward bank-rupting the middle class. The cuts in services to middle-class programs were justified by the budget deficit and national debt. Can you think of a more effective way to finish the job of eliminating the middle class than forcing the nation into bankruptcy? If you can, consider keeping it to yourself.

These fifteen steps have worked together to move the United States from a middle-class democracy to a corporate feudal republic. How did you do at crafting a smarter plan than this one? If you didn't think of a better way to accomplish the transition, remember that the one used by the Corporate Feudalists was perfected over the past thirty years. If, on the other hand, you happen to be among those who believe the decline of the middle class occurred by chance, consider this: What are the odds that all fifteen steps just happened to work together so seamlessly that even in hindsight it would be very difficult to improve upon them to achieve the same results? At the very least, we have to admit that the outcome is pretty fortunate for the top 1 percent.

PART THREE

The Current Landscape

CHAPTER 21

Newt Gingrich and the Republican Contract with America

During the introduction of the plan for Corporate Feudalism, Ronald Reagan played the part of the good cop. Grandfatherly and charming, how could anyone that nice be up to something as sinister as eliminating the middle class? On the other hand, Newt Gingrich played the part of the bad cop. He did not know how to play nice, and he didn't want to. Apart from Ronald Reagan, no one did more to publicly promote Corporate Feudalism than Newt Gingrich, who is responsible for three major contributions to the promotion of Corporate Feudalism.

First, in the 1980s Gingrich led the way in poisoning the atmosphere on Capitol Hill, changing the tone from collegiality to hostility, thereby teaching people to hate their government. Second, he and other members of the Republican Party authored the Republican Contract with America, a document designed to simultaneously elect conservatives to Congress and further the goals of Corporate Feudalism. Third, Gingrich successfully elevated Ronald Reagan to the position of a political saint. In addition, he was also perhaps the biggest hypocrite in Washington, DC, at a time when the competition both inside and outside of government had never been stiffer.

Before delving into the specifics of all Gingrich has done to destroy the US middle class and promote Corporate Feudalism, let us give him his due. Whereas Reagan was the movie star mouthpiece reading someone else's lines, Gingrich has been largely responsible for his own success. This is not to suggest that he acted alone. He both created and traded ideas and strategies with Grover Norquist, Dick Cheney, Arthur Laffer, and other politicos who have worked tirelessly to destroy the US middle class. But even in such esteemed company Gingrich stands out. He possesses a combination of leadership skills, intellectual brilliance, and unrestrained ambition rarely found in one individual, and he has applied these skills both tirelessly and, some would say, ruthlessly for much of his adult life.

The first of Gingrich's three major contributions to the promotion of Corporate Feudalism was changing the political tone in Washington, DC. Prior to his twenty-year tenure, from 1979 to 1999, Congress was like a club—a mostly white men's club, but a club nonetheless, where Republicans and Democrats argued during the day and socialized at night. The civility was noticeable, and it exerted a large impact on how things were done on Capitol Hill. But Gingrich realized that there was no way for the Republicans to regain control of Congress as long as such collegiality remained.

For forty years Democrats had controlled the House of Representatives, and there was no perceived change on the horizon. This was largely because most people were basically satisfied with their country and its direction. The US middle class had prospered and grown more in this forty-year period than at any other time in the country's history. Gingrich, through his leadership, changed all that. He convinced voters to be angry. He convinced voters to be dissatisfied. In the end, he convinced voters to hate their government.

The hate that Gingrich preached was aimed first at the Democrats. Instead of being part of the club called Congress, Gingrich used a club against Congress. He led the charge to turn partisan politics into warfare. For Gingrich and his followers, compromise and congeniality were signs of weakness not to be tolerated.

Gingrich's side planned the attack in secret and invaded without warning, similar to how the Vikings attacked a village or monastery in days gone by, the element of surprise often lasting long enough to ensure victory. Here was a collegial body being attacked ruthlessly from within. As they had with Reagan, the Democrats reacted to the changes Gingrich made with surprise and consternation. The Democrats and moderate Republicans stood by haplessly as the institutions they believed in were changed from collegial bodies where the nation's work was done to partisan battlegrounds where war was waged and protecting the interests of the United States was far less important than scoring political points.

The first response of the Democrats was to use compromise and reason to counter this attack on how things traditionally had been done. But the Democrats, and even many moderate Republicans, were ill prepared for the warlike attitude of Gingrich and his followers. While the Democrats were unwilling to call Reagan a liar even when it was blatantly obvious, Gingrich and his followers were more than willing to quickly label any Democrat who made a mistake or disagreed with them too strongly a liar. Gingrich and other Corporate Feudalists realized that the only way they could promote a truly radical agenda was to do it without warning or compromise. A simple change in political tone can have dire consequences, leading directly to the kind of gridlock often seen today in Congress.

Gingrich's second major contribution to the promotion of Corporate Feudalism was coauthoring the Republican Contract with America in 1994. The contract, a clearly intentional misnomer, was a fraud at best and a nail in the coffin of the middle class at worst. Based on what seemed to be common sense, the contract was designed to appeal to the general public, and it did. By signing the contract, members and wannabe members of Congress were openly proclaiming to be accountable to voters in a way that, according to them, had long since disappeared, if in fact it had ever existed.

The Republican Contract with America laid out, in very clear terms, much of the Corporate Feudalist agenda. It was a superior marketing tool, and Gingrich was a great salesman. Following is the Republican Contract with America in its entirety, with the exception of bill texts and descriptions.

Republican Contract with America

As Republican Members of the House of Representatives and as citizens seeking to join that body we propose not just to change its policies, but even more important, to restore the bonds of trust between the people and their elected representatives.

That is why, in this era of official evasion and posturing, we offer instead a detailed agenda for national renewal, a written commitment with no fine print.

This year's election offers the chance, after four decades of one-party control, to bring to the House a new majority that will transform the way Congress works. That historic change would be the end of government that is too big, too intrusive, and too easy with the public's money. It can be the beginning of a Congress that respects the values and shares the faith of the American family.

Like Lincoln, our first Republican president, we intend to act "with firmness in the right, as God gives us to see the right." To restore accountability to Congress. To end its cycle of scandal and disgrace. To make us all proud again of the way free people govern themselves.

On the first day of the 104th Congress, the new Republican majority will immediately pass the following major reforms, aimed at restoring the faith and trust of the American people in their government:

- **FIRST,** require all laws that apply to the rest of the country also apply equally to the Congress;
- **SECOND,** select a major, independent auditing firm to conduct a comprehensive audit of Congress for waste, fraud or abuse;
- **THIRD,** cut the number of House committees, and cut committee staff by one-third;

- **FOURTH,** limit the terms of all committee chairs;
- **FIFTH,** ban the casting of proxy votes in committee;
- **SIXTH,** require committee meetings to be open to the public;
- **SEVENTH,** require a three-fifths majority vote to pass a tax increase;
- **EIGHTH,** guarantee an honest accounting of our Federal Budget by implementing zero base-line budgeting.

Thereafter, within the first 100 days of the 104th Congress, we shall bring to the House Floor the following bills, each to be given full and open debate, each to be given a clear and fair vote and each to be immediately available this day for public inspection and scrutiny.

1. THE FISCAL RESPONSIBILITY ACT:

A balanced budget/tax limitation amendment and a legislative line-item veto to restore fiscal responsibility to an out-of-control Congress, requiring them to live under the same budget constraints as families and businesses.

2. THE TAKING BACK OUR STREETS ACT:

An anti-crime package including stronger truth-in-sentencing, "good faith" exclusionary rule exemptions, effective death penalty provisions, and cuts in social spending from this summer's "crime" bill to fund prison construction and additional law enforcement to keep people secure in their neighborhoods and kids safe in their schools.

3. THE PERSONAL RESPONSIBILITY ACT:
Discourage illegitimacy and teen pregnancy
by prohibiting welfare to minor mothers and
denying increased AFDC [Aid to Families with
Dependent Children] for additional children
while on welfare, cut spending for welfare
programs, and enact a tough two-years-and-out
provision with work requirements to promote
individual responsibility.

4. THE FAMILY REINFORCEMENT ACT:
Child support enforcement, tax incentives
for adoption, strengthening rights of parents
in their children's education, stronger child
pornography laws, and an elderly dependent
care tax credit to reinforce the central role of
families in American society.

**5. THE AMERICAN DREAM RESTORATION
ACT:** A $500 per child tax credit, begin repeal
wwof the marriage tax penalty, and creation of
American Dream Savings Accounts to provide
middle class tax relief.

**6. THE NATIONAL SECURITY RESTORATION
ACT:** No US troops under UN command and
restoration of the essential parts of our national
security funding to strengthen our national defense
and maintain our credibility around the world.

7. THE SENIOR CITIZENS FAIRNESS ACT:
Raise the Social Security earnings limit which
currently forces seniors out of the work force,
repeal the 1993 tax hikes on Social Security
benefits and provide tax incentives for
private long-term care insurance to let Older
Americans keep more of what they have earned
over the years.

8. THE JOB CREATION AND WAGE ENHANCEMENT ACT: Small business incentives, capital gains cut and indexation, neutral cost recovery, risk assessment/cost-benefit analysis, strengthening the Regulatory Flexibility Act and unfunded mandate reform to create jobs and raise worker wages.

9. THE COMMON SENSE LEGAL REFORM ACT: "Loser pays" laws, reasonable limits on punitive damages and reform of product liability laws to stem the endless tide of litigation.

10. THE CITIZEN LEGISLATURE ACT: A first-ever vote on term limits to replace career politicians with citizen legislators.

Further, we will instruct the House Budget Committee to report to the floor and we will work to enact additional budget savings, beyond the budget cuts specifically included in the legislation described above, to ensure that the Federal Budget deficit will be less than it would have been without the enactment of these bills.

Respecting the judgment of our fellow citizens as we seek their mandate for reform, we hereby pledge our names to this Contract with America.[1]

Newt Gingrich's Republican Contract with America demonstrates his brilliance and supports many of the points in the plan for Corporate Feudalism. Many people, especially conservatives, give him and his contract credit for the Republican recapture of the House of Representatives after forty years in the minority. But most people have not realized how important this document and the subsequent Republican majority were to destroying the US middle class and promoting Corporate Feudalism.

The brilliance of the Republican Contract with America is not difficult to see. It is short, easy to understand, and it appeals to common sense. It sounds like motherhood and apple pie all wrapped into one. However, when viewed in the context of the fifteen steps to Corporate Feudalism we can see how much this document does to legitimize the steps necessary to eliminate the US middle class.

The Republican Contract with America portrays a very dark state of affairs and implies the government is doing horrible things to its citizens. A close examination demonstrates how this is done through phrasing and suggestion. The first five lines of the contract include phrases designed to make people angry and influence them to hate their government. Examples are "to restore the bonds of trust," "era of official evasion and posturing," "the end of government that is too big, too intrusive, and too easy with the public's money," and "end the cycle of scandal and disgrace."

The eight reforms suggested are designed to show specific remedies. Although citizens don't really get much from them, it sounds like concrete action is being planned.

The first reform requires that all laws applying to the rest of the country will now apply equally to Congress. This insinuates that Congress has previously been considered to be above the law, which should make people mad. The second reform asks for a major, independent auditing firm to conduct a comprehensive audit of Congress for waste, fraud, and abuse—which, like calling for an investigation of child abuse, automatically raises suspicion about such failings. The third reform proposes cutting the number of House committees and committee staff by one-third, implying that there are too many congressional committees and too many staff members, resulting in government waste.

The fourth reform calls for term limits for all committee chairs, representing the initial salvo in the fraudulent conservative fight for term limits. The fifth reform bans the casting of proxy votes in committee, insider jargon that no one really understood but cast to make Congress look bad. The sixth reform requires committee meetings to be open to the public, pointing to a lack of accountability by members of Congress.

The seventh reform, which gets to the heart of Corporate Feudalism, requires a three-fifths majority vote to pass a tax increase. Note that there is no call for a three-fifths majority vote to pass a tax cut. According to this logic, if a simple majority passes a tax cut for billionaires and it turns out to be disastrous for the country, a simple majority cannot correct the error. This point reinforces the conservative myth that all taxes are bad and all tax cuts are good.

The eighth reform takes another shot at government in general by calling for an "honest accounting" of our federal budget by implementing "zero base-line budgeting." Zero baseline budgeting, however, has nothing to do with honest accounting, a reality that most citizens do not understand. Rather, zero baseline keeps large organizations spending most of their time and money working on the next year's budget. Could this be why a great corporate supporter like Newt Gingrich has not been able to convince a single large corporation to do zero baseline budgeting?

The real meat of the Republican Contract with America is outlined in the ten proposed bills. The one-sentence introduction continues the basic attack on Congress intended to arouse anger in the public. It calls for "full and open debate" with a "clear and fair vote" and each to be "immediately available this day for public inspection and scrutiny," implying that no such practices were in place prior to the contract.

The Fiscal Responsibility Act is essentially an attack on taxes, calling for a tax limitation amendment to restore fiscal responsibility to an out-of-control Congress.

The Taking Back Our Streets Act, supposedly an anti-crime bill, calls for "cuts in social spending...to fund prison construction," which furthers Corporate Feudalism by taking money away from members of the middle class and giving it to private, corporately controlled prisons.

The Personal Responsibility Act is aimed at taking money away from poor mothers and children "by prohibiting welfare to minor mothers and denying increased AFDC [Aid to Families with Dependent Children] for additional children while on welfare...." In addition to starving poor children, this law has the advantage of teaching middle-class citizens to hate the poor. The American middle class failed to realize this was the beginning of a plan that would eventually eliminate their government services as well.

The Family Reinforcement Act advances Corporate Feudalism by promoting tax incentives and credits as the answer to family problems, while attacking public education by calling for "strengthening rights of parents in their children's education." This act fails to name the rights the parents were lacking before it was proposed, but it clearly implies something was missing.

The American Dream Restoration Act is about cutting taxes and foreshadows the idea of turning Social Security over to Wall Street investors.

The National Security Restoration Act attacks the United Nations while calling for increased military spending.

The Senior Citizens Fairness Act advocates tax cuts, implying taxes are bad and tax cuts are good.

The Job Creation and Wage Enhancement Act uses the excuse of job creation to cut more taxes, including capital gains taxes that mostly affect the wealthiest Americans. Additionally, this act calls for deregulation in the form of "strengthening the Regulatory Flexibility Act."

The Common Sense Legal Reform Act is designed to limit the liability of corporations when they harm people, furthering the goals of Corporate Feudalism by allowing corporations more wealth and less accountability.

The Citizen Legislature Act is a conservative pledge for term limits. Although it commits to a vote only for term limits, when several signers of the pledge approached the appointed time to turn their house seats over to other citizen legislators, they realized that term limits weren't necessarily good after all.

In effect, the Republican Contract with America was a pledge to cut taxes (especially for the wealthy), eliminate regulations, reduce social programs, limit liability for corporations, and teach people to mistrust and hate their government. To a large degree, these goals were met and in many cases exceeded. The impact on the middle class was the opposite of everything promised, which, however, was no surprise to Gingrich or his cohorts.

The third of Gingrich's three major contributions to the promotion of Corporate Feudalism was elevating Ronald Reagan to the position of a political saint—a move with significant ramifications. Reaganomics was a magical illusion that promised lower taxes, a larger military, and a balanced budget. The problem for conservatives was how to maintain the illusion once the magician was gone.

What really happened during the Reagan presidency was very different from what conservatives claimed, as mentioned earlier. While Reagan cut taxes, particularly for the wealthy, he also left the biggest national debt in US history. He helped fund and train the Mujahedin in Afghanistan, including Osama bin Laden and others who went on to form the core of Al Qaeda. Reagan was also found guilty of violating international law by the International Court of Justice and ordered to pay reparations for his war against Nicaragua, which violated US law as well. In addition, Reagan gave weapons to our stated enemy Iran in exchange for the off-the-book and completely illegal favor of secretly transferring millions of dollars to the Contras in Nicaragua. All in all, the Reagan presidency was not the stuff legends are made of.

But if the goal was to perpetuate policies that were destroying the US middle class while transferring America's wealth to the top 5 percent of the population and leaving massive budget deficits in the place of a healthy economy, preserving the Reagan myth was essential. And Newt Gingrich was at the forefront of promoting this distorted version of the Reagan Revolution. Gingrich understood that, at least in the short term, the illusion of success was as important as success itself, so he and his minions continued to sell the Reagan myth long after Reagan was gone. Sometimes the claims were ridiculous, but Gingrich realized that if they were repeated often enough many people would believe them.

Conservatives praised everything about Reagan. They renamed Washington National Airport in Washington, DC, in Reagan's honor soon after he left office. Some even talked seriously about putting Reagan on Mount Rushmore with the "other great presidents." What had Reagan done to receive such adoration? Unless you happen to think budget deficits, illegal wars, and giving weapons to terrorists are the stuff of greatness, the answer is not much. So it is amusing is that even as the results of Reaganomics leave the US middle class at the door of extinction, Gingrich continues to advocate for the greatness of Ronald Reagan. Clearly he and his allies want the US economy and middle class to fail.

In addition to Gingrich's three major contributions to Corporate Feudalism, he elevated hypocrisy to new levels. Like other major capitals, Washington, DC, is built on hypocrisy. No political party or politician can claim superiority when it comes to hypocrisy, but Gingrich proved that he could rise above his peers. He accomplished his greatest acts of hypocrisy while serving as Speaker of the House in the House of Representatives, yet, like other conservative politicians, he held himself up as exemplifying the moral backbone of the country.

One act of hypocrisy was creating the myth that conservatives were the party of financial responsibility, as his Republican Contract with America clearly states, and then proceeding to squander taxpayer money by zealously investigating and prosecuting President Clinton in what became the most vicious witch-hunt in the history of modern American politics. Newt Gingrich was not only the conservative leader of the House of Representatives during these seemingly endless special prosecutors and impeachment trials but he fully supported and, as Speaker, orchestrated the Clinton witch-hunt. The attacks on President Clinton started with the revelation of a supposedly illegal real estate deal dubbed Whitewater. But after spending millions of US taxpayer dollars the conservatives realized they had found nothing. Undeterred, Gingrich and the conservatives went further. If Whitewater wasn't illegal, surely something else Clinton had done was. For years the investigations continued, in what amounted to using a taxpayer-funded blank check to destroy President Clinton—a hypocritical action that did not reveal the Republicans to be the party of financial responsibility.

Ultimately, when all that their chief inquisitor could uncover was the possibility of consensual sex between two adults the Republicans went for broke. Never before had so much money been dedicated to investigating one individual. And never before had so little been found. But if sex was all Gingrich had on Clinton he would use sex. Consequently, Gingrich orchestrated the largest sex trial in US and, perhaps, world history. Because of Gingrich's zealous attack on Clinton, America's children were exposed to daily updates on oral sex, consensual sex, and anything else having to do with sex. Parents had the choice of keeping their young children away from all news programs or exposing them to way more than the parents wished to explain. Never before had such detail been part of the daily news cycle—another act of hypocrisy by the Republican who held himself up as a pillar of family values.

But the extent of Gingrich's hypocrisy was not known until years later, when it was revealed that while orchestrating the Clinton impeachment he himself was having sex with one of his congressional staff members despite being married to someone else. This type of hypocrisy demonstrates a profound disregard for decency and morality. Because of Gingrich's witch-hunt, part of Bill Clinton's legacy will always include Monica Lewinsky. As for Gingrich, thus far he has escaped the legacy of being dubbed the nation's biggest hypocrite. But no interview with him should ever be conducted outside of Foxaganda without identifying him as the hypocrite who exposed the nation to Clinton's sex life while having sex with one of his own staff members.

The remaining questions are: Why would Gingrich allow his conservative Congress to waste millions upon millions of dollars to attack Bill Clinton, a conservative Democrat? Why would he expose the nation's children to such sordid details after learning that his inquisitor-in-chief could only find the possibility of consensual sex? How could he have had any part in this investigation when he was cheating on his own wife at the time?

Most likely the answer to these questions is that it was all about Corporate Feudalism. Clinton had reversed many—but not all—of the worst economic policies of the Reagan administration. He had raised taxes on the top 1 percent while cutting several taxes for lower-income individuals and families. He had reduced unemployment and the number of Americans living below the poverty line. He was reducing the nation's huge debt accumulated by Reagan and George H. W. Bush. He had created the largest budget surplus in history. Clinton had put forward an economic agenda and budget against which conservatives like Gingrich had fought furiously, claiming it would destroy the US economy. Instead, the economy was doing much better than it had under President Reagan or President George H. W. Bush. And all of this Clinton economic progress took place with absolutely zero Republican votes. Not one Republican in either house voted in favor of the economic policies that turned the nation's economy from the record-setting Reagan and Bush deficits to the Clinton surplus. At some point, people were going to realize that Reagan's crazy ideas were hurting the economy and the US middle class. But suddenly the stories about Clinton's economic success and its comparison with the Reagan and Bush deficit disasters disappeared, and all we heard about were the investigations of Clinton and his sex life. Thus, the attacks on Clinton kept the Reagan economic myth alive and allowed the plan for Corporate Feudalism to continue uninfluenced by the facts.

CHAPTER 22

A Brief Look at the Tea Party Movement

There are really two Tea Parties. The largest one is made up of angry, disgusted people who have finally had enough of the decline of the American middle class. The other one consists of corporate backers who want to make sure someone other than Corporate Feudalists are blamed for the demise of the middle class and growing wealth and income disparity among US citizens.

The first important thing to know about the Tea Party movement is that it was created, nurtured, and manipulated by the same people who created Foxaganda. For the first time in US history, a major television network was used as an organizing tool to spawn an American political movement. Well before there was a Tea Party movement, Foxaganda was publicizing it. In the old days, the establishment of a political organization or movement came first, followed by media coverage. With the Tea Party, however, nationwide media coverage came first, followed by the movement itself.

A second significant aspect related to the inception of the Tea Party movement is the fact that large amounts of corporate money were quietly and secretly funneled into various national organizations to help launch and organize it. The movement's national leadership consisted of major players in conservative politics, including owners of large corporations, as well as lobbyists and conservative politicians themselves.

A third important fact about the Tea Party movement is that every major candidate supported by the Tea Party has had an extremely procorporate agenda. What Tea Party members said they wanted was greater accountability and fiscal responsibility from their politicians. However, what they were conned into supporting by corporate-funded groups, conservative politicians, and Foxaganda was often the opposite of what they thought they were getting.

A look at several of the candidates backed by the Tea Party in the elections of 2010 is telling. That year, the Tea Party supported New York gubernatorial candidate Carl Paladino, who was caught forwarding to his friends, with his personal comments attached, some of the most graphic pornography available. In Florida, Rick Scott, the Tea Party–backed candidate, was one of the great perpetrators of the private health insurance fraud against senior citizens and the US government. He was elected governor of Florida with Tea Party support even after taking the Fifth Amendment seventy-five times in a single deposition during a fraud investigation in which the company he ran was found guilty of fourteen felonies and fined $1.7 billion. In the 2010 US Senate election in Alaska, the Tea Party supported Republican Joe Miller, who was caught lying and misusing other people's computers in an attempt to influence a different election. In Delaware, Tea Party candidate Christine O'Donnell—who had no experience in anything other than occasionally appearing on television—was caught lying about her education and allegedly used campaign contributions to pay her rent and other non–campaign-related expenses. In Nevada, Tea Party candidate Sharron Angle had to be kept away from the media after repeatedly saying wacky things– including telling a group of Hispanic students that some of them looked Asian and openly suggesting Second Amendment remedies that made some members of the Tea Party movement cringe. Indiana Republican Dan Coats, supported by the Tea Party as a "change candidate," was a former Republican sena- tor who had voted for the policies the Tea Party supposedly hated, only to leave government to become a bank lobbyist, lobbying for the very laws that have brought the nation's economy and the middle class to the brink of disaster. What all of these Tea Party candidates shared was a blatantly procor- porate agenda, a desire to leave Bush's tax cuts for billionaires in place and make them permanent if possible, and a drive to reverse health-care reform.

The blatantly procorporate agenda advocated by George W. Bush and the Republicans from 2000 to 2008 led the country directly into the economic disaster of 2008, which is said to have inspired the creation of the Tea Party. The tax cuts for billionaires advanced by Bush and the Republicans in 2000 were supposed to create jobs and stimulate financial growth, but the ten years following the passage of these tax cuts led to the largest recorded job losses since the Great Depression and the largest recorded budget deficits and national debt in US history. While health-care reform was vilified to the point of frenzy by Tea Party leaders, the independent, bipartisan Congressional Budget Office, regularly quoted and used by Republicans on other issues, found that the health-care reform measures passed by Congress would actually reduce the nation's deficit by $118 billion over the first ten years.

How were Tea Party members convinced to support policies that resulted in the opposite of what they said they wanted—fiscal responsibility, a lower deficit, and increased accountability? How were Tea Party members so easily convinced to support e-mail porn distributors, liars illegally attempting to influence elections, leaders in health insurance fraud, and laughing-stock candidates with no knowledge or experience in good governance and accountability? All it took to market and even elect some of the most anti–middle-class Congresspeople in recent memory was loads of cash and a great public relations campaign.

One unknown about the Tea Party is how long it will last. Will corporate sponsors pull their funding and let the Tea Party movement fade into obscurity or will Tea Party backers keep it going indefinitely? What is known is that if the Tea Party movement is allowed to die out its corporate sponsors will need to create another organization with the same purpose. As long as there continues to be a US middle class, Corporate Feudalists will need to keep the fear and anger of the middle class clearly directed at something other than themselves.

We have looked at the road map used by conservatives for the past thirty years to destroy the US middle class, and we have examined how the middle class was kept from seeing what was happening. Now that all of the steps, except for nationwide bankruptcy, have been fully implemented, members of the middle class see the writing on the wall. They may not know exactly what is taking place, but they know enough to realize that they are in serious trouble. They can no longer be fooled into believing that another tax cut for the very wealthy will save their jobs.

Today, throughout the entire country a quiet desperation has taken hold of much of the middle class. Each individual hopes that his or her job is not the next one to go. The children of middle-class parents are graduating from college only to discover that there are no jobs available for them. Families hope their children are fortunate enough to secure jobs that can at least pay off their student loans and provide for themselves and their families. Fear and anger are present everywhere. The question is where to direct this fear and anger. Who will the middle class blame for its demise? When one group or another was in trouble, it seemed easy to blame that group for its problems. But now that it's the entire middle class, who will shoulder the blame? If the Corporate Feudalists get their way, it won't be them. They have not worked on their plan this long only to get caught in the end. Now that it is impossible to convince the middle class that things are okay, the Corporate Feudalists need a pressure release valve, as well as a few scapegoats. This is where the Tea Party movement comes in.

The Tea Party movement is the first in what will no doubt become a series of efforts by Corporate Feudalists to redirect middle-class anger away from conservatives and their actions. The majority of the Tea Party members are middle-class citizens. They know their families are in serious trouble. Fearful and angry, they see their way of life slipping away and cannot figure out how they got into this position or how to get out. They worked hard and they followed the rules, as they understood them. At the same time, the Corporate Feudalists are more than willing to spend millions of dollars giving the middle class the billionaire spin on what happened. This is not meant to criticize people who have attended Tea Party meetings or consider themselves Tea Party members. They are scared and angry, and they have good reasons to be.

What Tea Party members are angry about is rather interesting, however. After the Supreme Court coup of 2000, the country experienced the longest running control of the US government by conservative Republicans in living memory. George W. Bush's presidency lasted eight years, during which all fifteen steps of the plan for Corporate Feudalism were, to one degree or another, implemented. For six of those years, both houses of Congress were controlled by committed conservatives who served as a rubber stamp for the Bush administration's agenda and the plan for Corporate Feudalism.

What did the middle class receive from this unprecedented conservative Republican rule? They received one of the largest tax cuts for the wealthiest citizens in the country's history. They obtained the largest budget deficit in actual dollars in the history of the world. They became involved in a war based on intentional lies and misinformation. They got the least regulated banking and mortgage industries in any living person's memory. And they witnessed the largest disparity in wealth and income between the upper class and the middle class since the establishment of the US middle class. But by the end of the Bush administration the middle class had inherited a housing and banking crisis that, according to President George W. Bush, would have bankrupted the United States and perhaps the world economy without his huge emergency bank and Wall Street taxpayer-funded bailout.

Yet throughout the entire time that the plan for Corporate Feudalism was being implemented, there was no public outrage and no Tea Party movement. Somehow, for many Tea Party members, out-of-control deficit spending for unnecessary wars and the banking deregulation leading to the largest home foreclosure rate since the Great Depression were not enough to get people out of their seats. A completely unregulated and unaccounted for infusion of nearly 5 trillion taxpayer dollars to Wall Street corporations couldn't even do it. While it is true that many people were openly angry about Bush's bank bailout, most were unable to connect the dots of the bank and mortgage deregulation and war spending with the economic collapse, particularly those who got their "news" from the Foxaganda network. What finally forced Foxaganda viewers out of their chairs and into the streets was the issue of providing health care to America's citizens.

Providing health care to Americans, like the care every other developed country in the world provides for its citizens, was the transgression that got the Foxaganda news-watching middle class to shout down their congressional representatives with such demands as "Keep the government out of my Medicare" during the Tea Party protests of 2010. Why? Because Foxaganda said so.

Since it is no longer possible for Corporate Feudalists to convince the middle class that things are okay, the conservatives' new strategy is to keep the middle class angry and fearful about health care and other things that might help the middle class so that it will not examine the policies of Corporate Feudalism that are leading to its destruction. Millions who have been misled are more than ready to be given easy answers to what ails them. The longer it takes the middle class to see what is happening to them and why, the more likely it is that the changes Corporate Feudalists have implemented will become irreversible. In effect, the Corporate Feudalists hope that if the public's anger could be directed away from the conservative policies that have been destroying the middle class they could continue their march toward Corporate Feudalism undeterred by an angry middle class.

While the task of the Tea Party movement has been to direct the fear and anger of middle-class citizens at their decline away from the top 1 percent of the population who have been quietly scooping up all of America's net worth for the past thirty years, the Occupy movement has completely refocused the debate. No longer is it concentrating on the corporately funded Tea Party, which blames everyone except giant corporations and the laws and tax policies that favor the top 1 percent; now middle-class citizens are increasingly hearing about the swelling income disparity in the United States and how the system has been rigged against the 99 percent of the population without access to their own team of lobbyists. The Occupy movement represents the first concrete proof that the Corporate Feudalists' plan of creating the Tea Party to divert attention away from themselves and their strategies has finally failed.

It remains to be seen how the Corporate Feudalists will further refocus the debate away from themselves and their strategies so middle-class citizens do not blame them for the decline of the middle class. No doubt their method will be clever, well funded, and completely supported by conservatives and the Tea Party movement. Maybe they will create another Tea Party–like movement. Or perhaps they will try something completely different. Whatever they do is sure to be hard, if not impossible, to trace back to the Corporate Feudalists themselves since they have plenty of money to cover their tracks.

CHAPTER 23

The Use of Fear, Anger, and Greed As Motivators

In our examination of the Corporate Feudalists' plan to destroy the US middle class, we have discovered why the middle class is no longer necessary to the Corporate Feudalists at the top of the economic ladder. We have discussed the origins of the middle class and why it was essential for those at the top to allow a middle class to come into being in the first place. Putting ourselves in the shoes of the Corporate Feudalists, we have seen how they created a fifteen-step plan that continues to be successful at eliminating the US middle class and turning our nation into a corporate feudal republic. But we still need to consider what motivated the middle class to help further this agenda.

Your goal now is to figure out how to motivate a large segment of the middle class to embrace the agenda of the Corporate Feudalists. The Corporate Feudalists themselves used fear, anger, and greed as their motivators. See if you can think of something better.

Prior to the Reagan Revolution, there was no real need to motivate the middle class to change, because there were no life-threatening issues facing them. The country was at peace—the Vietnam War had ended and the civil rights struggles were at low ebb. There were problems, of course. The US economy had sputtered, and interest rates had reached double-digit levels. The original energy crisis had hit, but President Carter had initiated a program of conservation and alternative energy development aimed at eliminating the country's dependence on foreign oil. Basically the US middle class was fat and happy when the Reagan Revolution began.

At that point, politics in the United States changed dramatically. And subsequently every policy and plan proposed or implemented by conservative Republicans could be seen through the lens of fear, anger, and greed. For the past thirty years, at least one of these three motivators has been used by conservatives to manipulate the middle class into accepting various public policies directly opposed to their own best interests.

At no time in US history prior to the Reagan Revolution had fear, anger, and greed been used so consistently and so effectively to motivate public policy. Because these tactics had never before been used so blatantly, both the public and non-conservative political leaders were caught off guard. The rules of the game had changed, but only the conservatives were aware of these changes and thus able to exploit their newfound power. The conservatives' first assault against the American public using these motivators was launched prior to Reagan's presidency with a group called the National Conservative Political Action Committee (NCPAC). This group created and funded a series of political ads based on fear, anger, and greed that were so misleading that the Democrats they targeted did not even bother to respond. Their failure to respond was believed to have contributed to the nearly unprecedented losses of several incumbent Democratic senators in the election of 1980.

The NCPAC's success proved to conservatives that fear, anger, and greed could successfully be employed to motivate middle-class voters and sway elections. While the Democrats learned that they had to respond to even the most outrageous and blatantly false attacks from conservatives, it took liberals many more years to realize that conservatives were intentionally using fear, anger, and greed to motivate the middle class. To this day, many liberals seem unaware of the extent to which conservatives employ these tactics to further their political agenda.

To demonstrate just how pervasive the fear, anger, and greed have become in conservative politics over the past thirty years, let's examine their involvement with each of the fifteen steps in the plan for Corporate Feudalism.

Step One: Controlling the Media

Controlling the media was one of the first steps taken to implement Corporate Feudalism without public knowledge or support. Through manipulation, intimidation, and consolidation, conservatives were able to gain control of the mainstream media's agenda while, at the same time, convincing the public that the mainstream media were liberal and not to be trusted.

Even in this case, where conservatives neither needed nor sought public support to achieve their goals, they used anger to further their objectives. For thirty years, conservatives have maintained that the news media have had a severe liberal bias, a claim that they have been able to use advantageously in at least two ways. First, the Corporate Feudalists used to their advantage the fact that a large segment of the US population no longer believes—and in some cases has contempt for—the real news media. This group, ultimately persuaded to no longer believe the real news media, unknowingly makes up part of the base of support for the Corporate Feudalist agenda. Second, the Corporate Feudalists used to their advantage the fact that many people who believe the real media have a liberal bias have turned to the well-funded conservative propaganda machine masquerading as news, and thus have become convinced that conservative propaganda is the real news.

As a result, a large group of US citizens accepts as true ideas proffered by conservatives that have, in fact, been proven false. For example, many people still believe that Saddam Hussein was involved in the 9/11 attack on the World Trade Center. Likewise, the same group of people who did not trust the real US media but were connected to the conservative propaganda network in the United States believed that Saddam Hussein had weapons of mass destruction before the Bush-led invasion and worked with Al Qaeda on terrorism projects aimed at the United States—even after both claims had been thoroughly investigated and proven false in the US and the international media.

As US media coverage of the lead-up to the Iraq war proved, regardless of how conservative the mainstream media became it was attacked as liberal by conservatives. For thirty years, the American public has been told that the mainstream media had lied to them. The resulting anger has allowed conservatives to convince a large segment of the population that up is down and black is white.

Step Two: Rush Limbaugh and "Foxaganda"

While fear, anger, and greed are powerful motivators, they could never have gained a strong foothold among US middleclass citizens without the twenty-four-seven sales job of Rush Limbaugh and Foxaganda. Take any issue and examine it from the perspective of fear, anger, and greed while listening to Limbaugh or watching Foxaganda and you will learn why you should be afraid and angry and why you would have a lot more money in your pocket if you simply followed the agenda of Corporate Feudalism. In Limbaugh's world, liberals are out to destroy your freedom and take your religion; environmentalists are secretly trying to turn the country into a communist dictatorship; and gays want to convert your children. Listening to Limbaugh or watching Foxaganda, you hear why you should fear the Democrats and liberals for wanting to increase taxes on billionaires and reregulate the banking and mortgage industry. After all that has happened to the economy under conservative Republican rule, Limbaugh and Foxaganda are still scaring people with tax-and-spend liberalism. And as long as large numbers of people continue to view this conservative propaganda as news there will be no way to break the cycle of fear, anger, and greed.

Step Three: Destroying the Unions

The Corporate Feudalists' use of fear, anger, and greed as motivators has been particularly effective with regard to the middleclass view of unions. For the last thirty years, conservatives have blamed the unions for just about everything. Despite the fact that there would have been no middle class in the United

States without unions, middle-class people have been taught to despise unions, and many in the middle class now view unions with contempt. They are afraid that unions will eliminate their jobs. They are angry with union workers, who supposedly make too much money and receive too many benefits. Conservatives claim that unions, by demanding higher wages and good benefits, caused jobs to be sent overseas. They also associated unions with protecting supposedly overpaid and underworked teachers in the public schools and being responsible for inflation whenever it occurs. In addition, conservatives have convinced the middle class that unions are taking money out of their pockets through increased consumer prices. By contrast, prior to the Reagan administration the middle class looked to unions to lead the way in increasing salaries and benefits.

Step Four: The Magic of Tax Cuts

Fear, anger, and especially greed have been used as motivators in teaching the American public to despise all taxes. The arguments conservatives have used to convince the middle class to hate taxes are similar to the arguments utilized to teach people to hate government. According to conservatives, taxes are bad because they take money out of your pocket. More money is good, and therefore taxes are bad. This is a misleading argument, perhaps, but simple to understand and, more importantly, effective in convincing the American public that reducing taxes for even the wealthiest individuals and corporations is good for them and for the US economy.

For the last thirty years, conservatives have claimed that the choice is between government waste and more money in your pocket. The argument is never "more taxes versus more services" or "more taxes versus better infrastructure," for example. Here again the tactics of fear, anger, and greed have played a significant role in the Corporate Feudalists' strategy to manipulate the American public into supporting economic policies that, while lining Corporate Feudalists' pockets, slowly contributed to the demise of the US middle class.

Step Five: Teaching People to Hate Their Government

All three motivators of fear, anger, and greed have been used to teach middle-class citizens to hate their government, which required greater motivation than teaching them not to trust the real media. The Corporate Feudalists have made every effort to change the American public's perception of their government from serving as a protector of their standard of living and safety to being an enemy of the people.

The Reagan administration's attacks on government workers were designed to instill fear and anger in the American electorate. According to Reagan, government bureaucrats were just sitting around finding ways to punish hardworking taxpayers for being good citizens or were finding ways to waste more of the public's taxpayer dollars. The majority of the conservatives' attacks on government centered on government waste. By framing their argument in terms of government waste instead of government service, conservatives have convinced many Americans that they could somehow pay fewer taxes while continuing to receive the same services. For more than thirty years, this something-for-nothing argument has successfully played directly into people's greed, but it has also had a very destructive impact on how people view their government.

Step Six: Privatizing ("Piratizing") Government

Greed is the primary motivator Corporate Feudalists have used to trick the American public into supporting the privatization of government services. Starting with the Reagan administration and continuing to this day, the American public has been told that any program run by the government could be run much more effectively and inexpensively by private corporations. Conservatives have claimed that while government bureaucrats intentionally wasted taxpayer money, private businesses could save taxpayers millions and even billions of dollars. Each conservative attack on bureaucrats made people angrier with their government, while praise for private business made the idea of privatization seem that much better. The choice was made to look simple: you could throw your taxpayer dollars away by allowing government bureaucrats to get their hands on your money or you could save billions by giving the taxpayer money directly to streamlined, profit-driven corporations that would do the work in place of the government. The promise of getting more money in your pocket without giving up anything in return has played successfully to people's greed.

Step Seven: Deregulating American Business
Every aspect of the conservative argument for deregulation of American business has been based on the motivators of fear, anger, and greed. A favorite claim is that government regulations destroy jobs. Given the fact that a middle-class life involves having a good job, the fear of losing it is a significant and legitimate concern. If regulations are seen as a vehicle used to destroy jobs, then deregulation would be seen as a vehicle used to create jobs. Environmental regulations, workplace safety regulations, and regulations of banks and Wall Street firms have all been cited by conservatives as reasons for the disappearance of good jobs in the United States.

According to the conservatives' rationale, because the government you have come to hate is responsible for the regulations that will make your job disappear, the logical response to government regulation is anger. Not only is your job at risk, but the entire US economy suffers as a result of these government regulations. Why wouldn't you, as a hardworking, responsible US taxpayer, be angry with a government that not only wastes your money but offers you nothing in return other than more needless regulations? It was asserted that government regulation equals money taken right out of your pocket, and without having to pay for unnecessary environment and safety regulations your employer would have more money to pay you.

Step Eight: The Global Free Trade Hoax

Greed has been the primary motivator used to sell the global free trade hoax as part of the plan to implement Corporate Feudalism. The motivators of fear and anger have been used in a more subtle and secondary way. The Corporate Feudalists' sales job was based on how much money people were supposedly going to save through supporting global free trade. For one thing, consumer prices would be lower, supposedly putting more money in American taxpayers' pockets. For another, the overall US economy would be improved by creating jobs for US workers who made products to sell to foreign countries.

Using fear as a secondary motivator, it was argued that jobs would be lost if the United States did not embrace global free trade, NAFTA, and other free-trade agreements proposed by conservatives. This fear of job losses was then used to fuel anger. According to the conservatives, anyone who did not support global free trade was working directly against creating jobs in the United States.

Step Nine: Destroying Public Education

Fear, anger, and greed have been used by conservatives to destroy public education. For thirty years, conservative leaders have told the American middle class that public school teachers are lazy, overpaid, liberal elite humanists who want to brainwash their children and that school administrators waste their money.

When the Reagan Revolution was unveiled thirty years ago, public education was very popular. But following the attacks on public education, people grew fearful about what their children were learning at school. They became angry with teachers and administrators. For many, the response was to pull their children out of public schools. For others, it was to organize efforts to reduce school funding and defeat school bond issues to teach these schools a lesson.

Consequently, the actual education of our nation's children has taken a back seat to the politics of education. While US public education was once seen as one of the best in the world, it is now viewed as inferior to the much more popular and successful programs of other developed countries. School board elections have become partisan battles over whether evolution or creationism should be taught in classrooms. Fights over allotting taxpayer money to private schools have become common. In just thirty years, public education has gone from being a popular program supported by nearly every American to being a hotbed of contention in local communities.

Step Ten: Promoting Unnecessary Wars

Fear and anger have been used by conservatives as motivators to launch and wage a series of unnecessary wars since the Reagan Revolution. Reagan used fear and anger to initiate the Contra War in Nicaragua, suggesting that the tiny country of Nicaragua was preparing to attack the United States via Mexico into Texas, a ridiculous belief that sparked fear in those who didn't know better.

During the administrations of both President George H. W. and President George W. Bush, these same motivators of fear and anger were used to launch both the first and second Gulf wars. By the time the lies about the supposedly precipitating circumstances were exposed, it was too late, for the wars were already underway. Fear and anger may have propelled us into these wars, but another great motivator—pride—kept us there. Many people felt we had to win, that our national pride was on the line.

In the case of the Iraq wars, even the real media became part of the cheerleading section for this aspect of the Corporate Feudalists' agenda, perhaps due to the motivator of patriotism, or maybe because the real media had learned its lesson after trying to give a somewhat more accurate picture during Reagan's war in Nicaragua. In either case, conservatives' use of war to promote their economic policies proved to be highly successful. By launching a series of unnecessary wars, they were able to effect yet another transfer of wealth from US middle-class taxpayers to the Corporate Feudalists.

Step Eleven: Conning the Evangelical Church

Fear and anger were used as motivators in the Corporate Feudalists' plan to con the Evangelical Church. According to the conservative narrative composed as part of the Reagan Revolution, the church was under attack by liberals and Democrats. So were American family values. In fact, church-goers were told that they had better fear secular humanist liberals or they would lose everything they held sacred because if liberals had their way, schools would teach their children all sorts of immoral things.

The Corporate Feudalists claimed that government rules and regulations would force people to go against their religious beliefs. These fear tactics aroused a great deal of anger in the American public, and millions of good Christian people came to feel that their way of life was under attack. Instead of trusting, as they had previously, that they could worship freely within the context of a diverse population, they were taught that they must use government to legislate their personal beliefs. Further, if they failed to legislate their own beliefs the godless liberals would turn their country into the next Sodom or Gomorrah.

The use of fear and anger as motivators to manipulate the Evangelical Church has led to the most faithful becoming the core of the Corporate Feudalists' support. But the fear of what they've been told and the anger that has been generated have blinded many to the realities occurring in their own middle-class lives and, more importantly, the party responsible for it.

Step Twelve: Developing a Policy of Lying

Fear, anger, and greed were not used to generate the lies that conservatives have espoused for the past thirty years, but were used to motivate middle-class support for the resulting policy of lying. Each step of the plan for Corporate Feudalism is based on a set of lies, some of which were easy to prove false. Over time, however, as these lies were systematically repeated and not exposed by the news media they started to seem real. With the necessary accountability missing in action, the resulting fear and anger promoted greed, and very soon these lies became reality for millions of middle-class citizens.

Step Thirteen: Exploiting Lack of Accountability

Because there never has been much political accountability in the United States, there was no need for Corporate Feudalists to use fear, anger, and greed to effectively exploit the lack of accountability. Nevertheless, conservatives have been extremely effective at generating anger among citizens by pointing out the lack of accountability involving Democrats while covering up their own lack of accountability. This can be seen clearly in the conservatives' somewhat successful efforts to blame President Barack Obama for the massive budget deficits created during the Bush administration at a time when both houses of Congress were controlled by conservative Republicans. Republicans have also successfully blamed President Obama and the Democrats for the Wall Street bailout, which was rushed through Congress during the final days of the Bush administration and caused by Bush's conservative economic policies—two "off the books" wars and massive billionaire tax cuts. Regardless of their claims, however, it remains apparent that the lack of accountability has led directly to the elimination of the US middle class and brought this country to the brink of Corporate Feudalism.

Step Fourteen: Corrupting the Courts

The main motivator used by conservatives to corrupt the courts was anger. By claiming that the courts were filled with liberals, conservatives managed to incite people's anger toward this supposed bias. Thus, when conservative ideologues were given court appointments, many people believed it was to reestablish balance.

Fear was not used directly to motivate a change in the Supreme Court, although a Supreme Court willing to use its power to appoint George W. Bush president when he had lost an election by more than half a million votes is one that should be feared. So is a Supreme Court majority willing to tell us the framers of the United States Constitution meant for corporations to have all of the rights of people but none of the responsibilities.

Step Fifteen: Bankrupting the United States

In all fourteen steps leading up to the possible bankruptcy of the United States, fear, anger, and greed have been used in various ways as motivators. More importantly, as the United States and state governments face bankruptcy Corporate Feudalists will use fear, anger, and greed to completely eliminate the US middle class. Glimpses of this can already be seen in the massive transfer of wealth that took place with the Bush bank bailout of 2008, the creation of the Tea Party movement in 2010, and the anti-union and anti-Medicare bills pushed at the state and federal levels in 2011.

Whether you are a Corporate Feudalist-in-waiting who has benefited from your regained position of wealth and power or a formerly middle-class worker who is fighting to survive on lower wages and fewer benefits as your country's economy crumbles around you, you can thank the Republican politicians and their conservative collaborators for bringing you to this place. If you are not one of the Corporate Feudalists-in-waiting, you must do everything in your power to overturn the fifteen steps in the plan for Corporate Feudalism now, while there remains a shadow of what once was the world's greatest middle class.

Conclusion: What's Next?

After reading about the plan for Corporate Feudalism, it is natural to wonder: What's next? But before creating a strategy to move forward, we need to carefully examine where we are. The first thing to realize is that the Corporate Feudalists have won this round. Their efforts over the last thirty years have succeeded. The middle-class democracy that made America great is in seemingly irreversible decline. The concentric circles of poverty will continue to grow as more and more formerly middle-class people will be unable to maintain their middle-class status. At the same time, the wealth of the top 1 percent will continue to increase at staggering rates of growth.

The second thing to understand is that incremental change will not bring back our middle-class democracy. The Corporate Feudalists have rigged the system in their favor to such a degree that the massive changes needed to restore the American middle-class democracy are completely out of reach using normal political channels. We cannot simply reverse the fifteen steps that brought us here and return to where we were. If we had a magic wand and could turn all of our legislators into true public servants like Senator Bernie Sanders or Congressman Dennis Kucinich, we would get the job done. But there are no magic wands, and the closest thing to one is the huge cash advantage Corporate Feudalists use to buy pro-corporate legislators and lobbyists.

Even so, we need not abandon the traditional political process. Using traditional political measures we can slow down the realization of Corporate Feudalism. People wanting instead to reverse this trend who are disappointed with President Obama might take into account the fact that during the administration of George W. Bush and the Republican-ruled Congress, the nation moved at breakneck speed toward Corporate Feudalism. During the Obama administration, progress continued but at a much slower pace. Although this is not what people hoped for when they voted for Obama and "change," it may very well be all that is possible at this country's current political juncture.

One change that may make a long-term difference is the Occupy movement, which has already altered the debate in the United States. By simply identifying the "99 percent" and the "1 percent," it opened the eyes of many middle-class Americans to a more accurate view of the wealth and income disparity between different groups of people in this country.

Another impetus for forward momentum will come from learning how the Corporate Feudalists succeeded in implementing their plan and then imitating their strategy and tactics. True, they have distinct advantages over middle-class citizens, but then middle-class citizens have a few advantages of their own.

How did the Corporate Feudalists nearly succeed in transforming our country from a middle-class democracy to a corporate feudal republic in thirty years? First, they had a goal—to replace middle-class democracy with Corporate Feudalism. Second, to accomplish this goal they created a plan that was radical, comprehensive, visionary, and not limited in any way by what seemed possible at the time. And third, they were able to convince a large segment of the population that their plan was good for the middle class and for America.

It's easy enough to state a new goal. Let's say our goal is to reverse Corporate Feudalism and the decline of America's middle-class democracy. Now we need to create a plan to accomplish this goal. Like the Corporate Feudalists' plan, it must be radical, comprehensive, visionary, and not limited by what seems possible. And it must contain specific steps for exactly how to accomplish it.

Throughout this book you have been asked to imagine what you would do, as a useful exercise to help see how the plan for Corporate Feudalism might look to the people benefiting from it. In addition, this exercise makes clear just how well thought out each part of the plan was toward accomplishing the overall goal of eliminating America's middle class. Used well, the exercise can also help stimulate answers to the question: What would you do to reverse the trend toward Corporate Feudalism and restore America's middle-class democracy?

Even when a goal is easy to identify, the steps necessary to accomplish it may not be. For example, one obvious step toward the goal of reclaiming middle-class democracy would be to change how political elections are financed in the United States. The "whoever spends the most money wins" system now in place clearly serves the interests of Corporate Feudalists. We might think we could accomplish this step by simply convincing legislators to change the system. But many of our legislators have already been bought and paid for by the Corporate Feudalists and benefit directly from the current system. We might consider appealing to the highest court in the land. But, as discussed earlier, the majority of the current justices of the Supreme Court already side with the Corporate Feudalists.

Consequently, to achieve our goal our task must be to formulate a plan outside the box that is not limited by what we think is possible and clearly lays out the changes we want to see. Efforts underway to amend the Constitution so it states that corporations are not people and to make public financing of campaigns the law of the land are examples of this approach.

Part of the brilliance of the Corporate Feudalists has been the way they set out to accomplish all of their steps at once. The plan to reverse Corporate Feudalism in order to return the 99 percent to a place of power will need to adopt this same strategy. Let's look at a few possible ideas for moving in this direction.

One idea is to eliminate voting and return to the original Athenian custom of election by lottery. The reason Athenians, the originators of democracy, used a lottery instead of a vote was because they feared elections could be manipulated by very wealthy or powerful families. A look at our current system shows that the Athenians were right: big money wins elections. While this system works great for people and corporations able to spend the amounts of money required to buy elections, it no longer works for ordinary people. If a lottery by congressional district were used for elections, housewives and plumbers would be as likely to be members of Congress as lawyers and millionaires.

Another idea for reversing the advance of Corporate Feudalism is to put a 90 or 95 percent tax on all lobbying, or even outlaw lobbing altogether. It's no secret that corporate lobbyists are having a significant negative impact on our democracy. The least we can do is insist they help pay for all their damage.

Yet another idea is for a massive public works program like those of FDR's era, including a project to build nationwide water pipelines crisscrossing the country to help alleviate at least some problems related to the effect of global climate change on the economy. Due to global climate change, the weather is much less stable than even a few years ago. We have seen an increase in the number and intensity of floods, droughts, fires, tornadoes, and hurricanes, and scientists say to expect this pattern to continue. Shipping water from overly wet areas to drought-stricken regions could reduce flooding, help end crop loss due to droughts, and give dry communities water for daily needs and to fight fires. A project this massive would also create jobs in every state in the nation for building, managing, and maintaining the water highway. It could be required, by law, that all equipment needed to complete this project be manufactured in the United States as well. The millions of jobs necessary to complete a project this large would be a game changer for America's middle class and would help restart the US economy. What would it take to initiate such a project, and how could we prevent the Corporate Feudalists and their political allies from privatizing it to reap excessive profits from it?

Another easy-to-imagine publicly funded project could be to end all oil and nuclear subsidies and use the money saved to install solar collectors on every residence in the United States. The benefits would include thousands, if not millions, of jobs in this country, a radical reduction of greenhouses gases, elimination of the need for more polluting power plants, and much more localized generation of electric power.

We know giant multinational corporations are destroying our middle-class democracy, so we need to consider how to limit the influence and power of such megacorporations and their owners. One idea is to limit the lifespan of megacorporations to twenty-five or fifty years, after which their assets would go to the US Treasury to benefit the US government. A second idea is to limit executive pay to a certain percent more per hour than the average worker at the same company, such as 15 or even 45 percent, instead of the 450 times more per hour currently paid to some CEOs. This restriction would bring pay equity more in line with that of other developed nations. A third idea is to require that all corporations with more than one hundred or even five hundred employees be unionized and that boards of directors be made up of workers and management. In addition, if we reversed global free trade and went back to the trade policies and tariffs in place before the Reagan Revolution we might be able to stop multinational corporations from benefiting at the expense of American workers. A fourth idea is to eliminate the megacorporation model completely in the United States. Maybe the opposite of "too big to fail" should be "too big to exist." A more moderate approach would be to return taxes on giant corporations and their millionaire owners to levels that preceded the Reagan Revolution, when the US middle class was thriving. A 75 to 90 percent tax on all income assets and dividends over $1 million per year might be reasonable.

A plan to reverse the trend toward Corporate Feudalism could emerge from the following ideas as well: publicly finance all political campaigns and outlaw all campaign contributions; reinstate the Glass-Steagall Act to reregulate the banking industry; create an independent board responsible for examining media accuracy and for stopping the media from using the word *news* if they are found to be consistently wrong or misleading; reinstate the fairness doctrine; begin Medicare single-payer health care for all citizens; provide free public education at all levels; reinstate trade protections to keep jobs in the United States; make all trade agreements reciprocal, ending the practice of letting a country maintain a different policy for imports and exports; stop exporting natural resources and only export finished products; abolish any law that gives corporations the rights of individuals without the responsibilities; punish political and economic criminals like the people whose lies got us into the wars in Iraq and created the housing crash; institute a mandatory national service requirement for all citizens; add an annual surtax to all estates worth more than $5 million; return to pre-Reagan tax rates; tax capital gains at the highest level;

change the 1872 mining law to recover fair return for government resources; and tax all transactions in the financial markets.

These are just a few of the ideas that should be considered. The important point is that the top 1 percent figured out a step-by-step plan to convince the middle class to eliminate themselves in thirty years, and now it is time for the 99 percent to develop a step-by-step plan to reverse this disastrous direction and restore America's middle-class democracy.

Reviewing the advantages and disadvantages of the Corporate Feudalists' strategy can help the 99 percent more clearly envision its own advantages and disadvantages. The main advantage the Corporate Feudalists have is their access to unlimited money. This has allowed them to create their own national television network and hundreds of smaller media outlets, as well as influence politicians at every level of our political system. One disadvantage the Corporate Feudalists have is the need to convince people that black is white and up is down, in order to hide the true goal of their plan from the middle class. This is why they need to create movements like the Tea Party to keep middle-class people from discovering the true causes of the decline of the middle class.

By contrast, the two most obvious advantages of people wanting to reverse the trend toward Corporate Feudalism and restore America's middle-class democracy are numbers and openness. The nature of Corporate Feudalism requires that a very small number of very powerful people and corporations control all the wealth and power, meaning that potentially 95 to 99 percent of the population, upon becoming more aware of what the Corporate Feudalists have done to America, could be mobilized to oppose them. The second advantage is that once the people who want to reverse the trend toward Corporate Feudalism have a plan, they don't have to hide it or pretend it is doing the opposite of what it's supposed to do. An obvious disadvantage for this same group is that they lack unlimited money and therefore cannot buy their own television network, major media outlets, or enough politicians to restore the middle class through legislative means.

We don't know which people or organizations created the plan for Corporate Feudalism in the first place. However, we do know what their plan has accomplished. We are aware of the legislators who have been behind it. And we can identify who benefits from it.

The challenge for those of us who are not part of the top 1 percent is to create a radical, comprehensive, and visionary plan to reverse the trend toward Corporate Feudalism and restore the middle-class democracy that made this country great.

What will you do?

Notes

Chapter 1

1. Image adapted by Jim C. Greevy using data from the US Treasury Department, Bureau of National Debt, http://jimcgreevy.com/gvdc/ NatlDebtChart.html, September 15, 2011.

2. Thomas Piketty and Emmanuel Saez, http://rwer,wordpress. com/2010/09/20/graph-of-the-week-the-top-10-income-share-in-usa-1917-2008/, September 15, 2011.

3. Image adapted by Working Thoughts from Andrew Sum and Tess Forsell, "Wealth in America: Who Gets What and How Wealthy Were the Forbes 400 Richest Billionaires in 2008 Relative to America's Bottom Half?" (2009). Center for Labor Market Studies Publications. Paper 19. http://hdl.handle.net/2047/d20000600, September 15, 2011.

4. Image created by Dennis Marker using data from *The Guardian*, UK, and *Forbes* magazine. http://www.guardian.co.uk/business/2010/ feb/16/wells-fargo-chairman-highest-us-earner http://www.forbes. com/lists/2009/12/best-boss-09_CEO-Compensation-Health-Care-Equipment-Services_9Rank.html.

Chapter 17

1. http://www.allhatnocattle.net/reagan%20quotes.htm.

Chapter 20

1. Naomi Klein, *The Shock Doctrine: The Rise of Disaster Capitalism* (New York: Picador, 2007).

Chapter 21

1. The Republican Contract with America, http://www.house.gov/house/ Contract/CONTRACT.html, September 15, 2011.

About the Author

During his career in Washington, DC, Dennis Marker worked for the US Congress, the administrator of the Environmental Protection Agency, various political campaigns, and Jim Wallis at *Sojourners* magazine. In addition, he helped launch and directed Washington, DC–based progressive nonprofits, including Witness for Peace and The Pledge of Resistance, where he specialized in national and international media operations. This work took him from every country in Central America to Iraq and many countries in between, where he negotiated with government officials and nongovernmental organizations looking for ways to avoid war and limit civilian causalities.

Marker has appeared on numerous network and cable television news and talk shows in the United States, Canada, Mexico, Australia, and throughout Europe. He has also been used as an on- and off-the-record source by many publications, including *Newsweek, Time, Business Week, The Wall Street Journal, The Nation, The Christian Science Monitor, The Washington Post, USA Today,* and other major newspapers in the United States and internationally. In addition, he has written, edited, and been the on-air voice for a weekly UPI-syndicated political radio commentary.

One Standard Press
PO Box 22690
Santa Fe, NM 87502
For book orders: www.thefifteensteps.com
For money puppets: www.moneypuppets.com